Rosa Nouchette Carey

Sir Godfrey's Grand-daughters

Vol. I

Rosa Nouchette Carey

Sir Godfrey's Grand-daughters
Vol. I

ISBN/EAN: 9783337040642

Printed in Europe, USA, Canada, Australia, Japan

Cover: Foto ©ninafisch / pixelio.de

More available books at **www.hansebooks.com**

SIR GODFREY'S GRAND-DAUGHTERS

A Novel

BY

ROSA NOUCHETTE CAREY

AUTHOR OF
'NELLIE'S MEMORIES,' 'LOVER OR FRIEND,' 'NOT LIKE OTHER GIRLS,' ETC.

IN THREE VOLUMES
VOL. I.

LONDON
RICHARD BENTLEY AND SON
Publishers in Ordinary to Her Majesty the Queen.
1892
[All rights reserved]

CONTENTS OF VOL. I.

CHAPTER	PAGE
I. DR. LYALL DISLIKES HIS SITUATION	1
II. FIVE MINUTES LATE BY GRANDFATHER'S CLOCK	17
III. BREAKING THE ICE	35
IV. 'HE IS A DEAR, GOOD FELLOW!'	56
V. A PAGE OUT OF THE HAMLYN RECORDS	74
VI. 'IT SHALL BE NOBODY'	96
VII. A TROUBLESOME PATIENT	116
VIII. WON BY THE MAJORITY	137
IX. ON THE CHILVERTON ROAD	158
X. AN INNOCENT MATCHMAKER	179
XI. GERARD FINDS HIS OPPORTUNITY	194
XII. 'YOU HAVE HELPED ME'	215
XIII. SIR GODFREY HAS A TOUCH OF GOUT	237
XIV. ST. JUDE'S VICARAGE	258
XV. TWILIGHT CONFIDENCES	277
XVI. PAMELA	297
XVII. 'WITH DR. AND MISS LYALL'S COMPLIMENTS'	313

SIR GODFREY'S GRAND-DAUGHTERS

CHAPTER I.

DR. LYALL DISLIKES HIS SITUATION.

'Vessels large may venture more,
But little boats should keep near shore.'
                    BENJAMIN FRANKLIN.

'My good sir, I must protest——'

'My dear sir, not a word! I will take no refusal; I will give no countenance to such a suicidal plan. Where are my people? Here!—Rogers, Stephens, one of you fellows —run up to the Hall, tell Mrs. Meredith that the bachelor's room is to be got ready for this gentleman: fire, hot water—she will understand. Look sharp! Don't stand there staring at me; off with you!—Now, my dear sir, take my arm and walk as fast as you can. Mind! the ground is slippery. I dare not take you by the short-cut; we should both come to grief. To be sure'—in answer to a mute response, very significant in its meaning—'I forgot your wet clothes. Shall I lead the way? We have only half a mile before us.'

What a ridiculous position! It was impossible to get in a word with this garrulous old gentleman. He was evidently master of the situation; he had turned a deaf ear to every remonstrance. Here was he, Dr. Lyall, delivered up, a shivering, unwilling captive, into the hands of this arbitrary stranger. What would Pamela say if she could see him now — his clothes dripping with water, his teeth chattering, dragging himself over the frozen ground at the heels of this nimble-footed and straight-backed old gentleman? Never before had he found himself in such an absurd predicament, and if there were anything that Dr. Lyall detested from the bottom of his heart, it was fuss, bustle, or commotion of any kind. He was a quiet man, self-restrained, and with a sense of humour; and though he was thankful enough for his escape, for he had been in a perilous position ten minutes before, and still more thankful that he had been of use to a human being, he could not help thinking of Pamela's amused countenance when she should hear all the ridiculous details.

Well, it had been touch and go at one moment—he hardly thought he could have lasted another minute, the girl was so terribly heavy. By-the-bye, he hoped she had reached the house by this time; her sister—he supposed it was her sister; how was he to know?—seemed to have a sensible head on her shoulders. Anyhow, he had done his duty. He had managed to gasp out his directions pretty plainly: ' Make her walk if she can; anyhow, get her to some house. She must have her things off at once, and go into a warmed bed; give her some brandy—I am a doctor—ah, there's a carriage!—all the better, she will be the sooner at home—rub well with warm towels, a hot bath if her limbs ache—don't let her stand a moment.' How had he contrived to make himself audible? But he had certainly heard, 'Thank you, oh, thank you so much; I quite understand,' in a clear young voice that sounded very near him.

But his host was speaking; worse than that, he was waiting for him. The path had widened; two men could walk abreast now.

'I hope you do not feel very much chilled,' in an anxious voice; 'there was so little brandy in that flask, hardly a mouthful—they gave some to Gerda. Do you think the shock will harm her?'—anxiety evidently on the increase. 'My grand-daughter has a very sensitive organization, but she was not so very long in the water, was she? Good heavens! what should we have done if you had not gone so quickly to her rescue? Providence must have brought you here — I think seriously on these subjects; I believe in a special Providence. We are deeply indebted to you for your presence of mind and your courage, we are indeed, and I am sure my daughter will endorse this. There is the Hall. We shall soon be up this hill; you walk stiffly, my dear sir, but of course your clothes are heavy.'

A grim smile crossed Dr. Lyall's face. In spite of his discomfort he could still realize the humour of the situation.

'That is the Hall, I suppose?' eyeing some tall chimneys dubiously.

'Yes, Chesterton Hall. Of course, if you are Captain Hake's friend, you will have heard my name,' drawing himself up a little proudly. 'We consider ourselves near neighbours.'

'I am afraid,' in an embarrassed voice, 'that I have not that pleasure. This is my first visit down here. Hake only came back from India two years ago, and I have never been able to accept his invitation before now. His wife was an old school-friend of my sister's.'

'Indeed!—a nice chatty woman; my granddaughters are very fond of her—humph!' with rather a dignified air: 'you must allow me to introduce myself—Sir Godfrey Hamlyn, at your service.'

'My name is Lyall—Dr. Lyall,' returned the younger man quietly, as he stole a glance at his companion.

What an aristocratic old fellow he was! No doubt in his youth he had been handsome: his features were fine and his complexion had the tint of old ivory; he was well preserved, too, in spite of the lines that were plainly visible; and any young man might envy his upright carriage. If only he could be silent a moment; but he was as fluent of tongue as a woman. What a blessing! there was the house at last — a gray weather-beaten-looking place, standing just outside the park gates, with rather an unpretending entrance; but somehow he liked the look of it, though he devoutly hoped that he would not have to encounter any more of the family. Of course there would be the servants about; there was the butler on the steps, evidently on the look-out for them. Sir Godfrey hailed him at once:

'Is the bachelor's room all ready, Dalton?'

'Perfectly ready, Sir Godfrey.'

'All right; show Dr. Lyall to his room at once—stop, I will take him myself: is Mr. Gerard in? No; well, let me know directly he arrives. Now then, my dear sir, this way'—disregarding his guest's remonstrance, 'Dalton,' still talking fast, 'send Rogers at once to Braeside for Dr. Lyall's Gladstone; his things have gone on there. Tell Captain Hake, with my compliments—my compliments, Dalton—that I am detaining his guest; let Rogers inform him of the accident—he was there and saw it all; there is no time to write a note.'

'My dear sir,' interposed Dr. Lyall, with just a trace of irritation in his quiet tone, 'please allow me to send a message. Tell Captain Hake,' addressing the man in rather a curt, authoritative voice, 'that I am only in need of some dry clothes; that I have taken no harm, and shall certainly be at his dinner-table this evening. That is all that need be said,' as Sir Godfrey shook his head. 'You are very good, Sir Godfrey, and these are comfortable quarters,' looking round the luxuriously-furnished room, and then at the fireplace, where some dry pine-logs were spluttering and blazing; 'but I do not mean to trespass on your hospitality for more than a few hours.'

There was a little more argument, a few pressing inquiries as to his physical feelings, some well-meaning advice, and then Sir Godfrey went in search of his daughter. He had not forgotten the other sufferer, who was his own flesh and blood; but the Hamlyns were hospitable people, and *noblesse oblige:* the stranger who had rescued his grand-daughter, who had risked his own life—Sir

Godfrey liked to put things in their strongest light—had undoubtedly the first claim on him. Sir Godfrey, with his old-fashioned courtesy, his punctilious, chivalrous notions, would have willingly served him with his own hands if Dr. Lyall would have permitted it. It cost Dr. Lyall some trouble to get rid of him and Dalton. As soon as he was alone, he locked the door and drew a long breath of relief, and then set himself seriously to better his condition.

A few minutes later he sat by the fireside, warmly wrapped up in a quilted dressing-gown belonging to his host, sipping a stiff glass of brandy and water. A hot bath had refreshed him; he had an eider-down over his knees, never in his life had he felt more comfortable, and, blessing of blessings, he was alone: not even Sir Godfrey would force his way through a locked door—why, he had even drawn the bolt between him and the outer world.

So this was the bachelor's room—bachelors were in clover at Chesterton Hall; but how did Sir Godfrey guess that he was an unmarried man? He looked old enough and staid enough for a Benedict; but a truce to this nonsense! he must set himself to review the whole situation. How many hours was it since he had left Pamela, and had nodded and waved to her? Hours—tut! it was barely an hour and a half, and yet all this had happened. She had merely nodded in an off-hand way as she settled herself against the cushions of the carriage, he believed she had not even looked at him; and yet at one moment—one confoundedly unpleasant moment—he thought he should never see her again.

Sir Godfrey believed in a special Providence, did he? Good old man! on the whole he shared his opinions; but he was an Englishman, and preferred to keep all such opinions to himself.

Now for it—he must go over the whole thing point by point before he got sleepy; but the fire was warm and the brandy was potent. He wondered if the young lady were asleep by this time.

Well, after all, it was a droll idea of his to stop the carriage and insist on walking the remainder of the way. It was a good two miles to Braeside, the coachman told him, but he was cold and wanted to stretch his legs, and Pamela could take care of herself and the luggage.

She did not really mind, though she grumbled, and told him he would get cold tea, and most likely lose his way; but she was accustomed to be overruled by his masculine will, and she would only revenge herself by a little quiet satire at his expense afterwards.

He had enjoyed his walk very much, and he fancied he was near his destination, when, by either good or ill luck, he saw some boys with skates slung over their shoulders, and on questioning them found out that they were going to skate on the lake in Chesterton Park.

'Anyone goes who likes,' one of the boys informed him. 'There is rare good ice, and the Squire takes no end of trouble about it. People come from miles round, and it is quite lively sometimes;' and then they had wished him good-afternoon and had gone on their way.

He could not imagine what put it into his head to follow them; he was excessively fond of skating, and as a holiday was a rare thing in his hard-working life, he determined to make the most of it; perhaps Hake would be there himself, and gentlemen were not wanted at afternoon tea—it was the women's hour. Perhaps it was as well for the young lady that he had yielded to the temptation. He felt rather like a truant school-boy as he turned in at the park-gates; he scarcely noticed the gray old Hall as he passed it. The lads were before him, racing each other down the ice-bound path, and he had rather a difficulty to keep them in sight. Presently he caught a blue gleam through the trees, and, walking more slowly, he presently found himself at the edge of a little lake, which seemed to wind very prettily between thickly-wooded banks.

There were a great many skaters, and he stood still to watch them. Some of the ladies skated very gracefully. There were two rather tall girls among them; as they were dressed alike—in dark tweed dresses —he thought possibly they might be sisters.

One of them skimmed over the ice with a quiet grace that somewhat fascinated him— she was a pale, delicate-looking girl, with fair hair, that looked very nice under her close little velvet hat. The other girl skated very well too, but her movements were not so uniformly graceful. Somehow, he singled out these two girls, and watched them, half idly, half admiringly, after the manner of masculine loungers. There was nothing very remarkable about either of them; he had seen far prettier girls any day in London. The younger one had a round, innocent-looking face, and her hair looked rough and curly, as though the exercise had dishevelled it; and once or twice, as she shot past him, she looked at him with child-like curiosity, as though marvelling at the presence of a stranger. He thought the other sister had not noticed him at all, she was so intent on her amusement.

It was a raw wintry afternoon, and standing made him feel chilly. How he wished he had his skates with him! it was almost too tantalizing to watch other people enjoying his favourite pastime. To keep himself warm he walked briskly to the other end of the lake, where a couple of swans were pluming themselves discontentedly outside their little wooden house. The snow had not been so carefully cleared here, and it was evident that this part of the lake was not used by the skaters; to his practised eye the ice looked somewhat thin and unsafe.

'They ought to warn people not to come farther than that island,' he said to himself; 'to my mind, there is a treacherous look about the ice here. I don't believe it would bear my weight. What fools people are, not to take precautions! The Squire, whoever he is, is responsible for the safety of his guests. I have almost a mind to speak to someone. Hollo! by Jove! here comes one of those girls. I must warn her.'

Well, he had warned her—at least, he had tried to do so—but she had evidently not heard him. She was making the circuit of the lake. She swept round the farther bank, and then steered her course straight towards the point where he was standing.

'Don't come any farther; the ice will not bear!' he had shouted, and then she had stopped and looked at him in a half-hesitating way.

'It was quite safe yesterday,' she had returned. But before the words were out of her mouth there was a crash—a fissure—and then a terrified scream as the poor girl felt the deadly cold of the water closing round her.

'Save me! save me!' he heard her gasp, as her agonized hands tried to grip the breaking ice.

'Keep still; I will do all I can,' he had shouted. How had he managed to reach her? His memory failed to help him here. He fancied he had crawled on his hands and knees over the few feet of ice that lay between her and the bank. It was a terribly risky thing to do. The next moment he was in the water too, and was holding her up, and imploring her not to struggle. He was only just in time; he was sure of that. Another moment, and she would have been sucked under the ice. She was only half conscious too, and her weight nearly broke his arm.

He was pretty sure, in thinking it over, that the ground shelved just there. For one moment he had lost his footing, and seemed out of his depth. The next his head and shoulders were out of the water, and the girl's head was above water too; but it was all so confused, so sudden, so horribly unreal, that even now he hardly knew how it had all happened. Every moment the ice seemed breaking round him, the water grew more deadly cold, and his arm became more numbed. 'Good God!' he had said to himself, 'I cannot hold her a moment longer.' But even as the thought crossed him help had come.

His sharp cry for assistance had been heard. Men were running down the bank. A plank was held out to him. Thank Heaven! he had still strength to grasp it. Another moment, and they were both in safety, and a rough-looking man in the dress of a gamekeeper was holding a flask to his mouth.

'Take a good pull, sir. We have given the young lady some.'

And then he had found strength to gasp out his directions. He would have gone to her at once. Being a doctor, he felt bound to do so. But for the moment he was too numb to move, and he was reassured by seeing her pass him, supported by a gentleman, and wrapped in a fur-lined cloak. They were helping her into a carriage, and the girl he took for her sister followed her.

'The brandy has brought her round,' an old gentleman had assured him. 'Jamieson had his flask, luckily. Now, my dear sir, we must think of you.' And then had followed the brief argument, which had ended in victory on Sir Godfrey's side.

'Life is a curious thing,' he went on drowsily, as he ended this retrospect with a shiver. 'One never knows what comes in the day's work. When I packed up my Gladstone this morning to the tune of "Come, lasses and lads," it never entered my mind that I was to be half drowned before night. Faugh! it was an unpleasant situation;' and, in spite of his philosophy and his present comfort, Dr. Lyall gave a genuine shudder as he recalled the dead weight of the half-conscious girl, and how the icy cold of the water had seemed to deprive him of breath. 'It is a nasty feeling—that of a rat in a hole,' he thought. 'If one could strike out and swim, one would not mind a plunge in winter time. I have often heard of ice accidents, but I never realized them before. I wonder what Pamela thinks of my adventure. Of course, she will have her fun out of it—trust her for that!'

Here Dr. Lyall's thoughts became confused, and a few moments later he was fast asleep.

CHAPTER II.

FIVE MINUTES LATE BY GRANDFATHER'S CLOCK.

'Even his own tail is a burden to the weary fox.'—
Proverb of Montenegro.

A BRISK knock at the door, then another, still louder and more imperative. Dr. Lyall sat up and rubbed his eyes in rather a bewildered fashion. Had he been asleep? The room was nearly dark. A great red hollow had replaced the blaze. Dr. Lyall looked at it drowsily. Then he said:

'Come in.'

'I am afraid I must trouble you to unlock the door,' returned a cheerful voice which certainly did not belong to his host.

'Oh, I quite forgot the bolt,' with an apologetic laugh. 'I believe I have been asleep.'

'Upon my word, I believe so, too; and,

not being a disembodied spirit, I have not learnt the vanishing trick yet.'

This was decidedly frivolous. Sir Godfrey would certainly not express himself in this way. As he grappled rather clumsily with the lock, he wondered who the newcomer would be. The next moment a tall, broad-shouldered young man walked into the room with a Gladstone bag in his hand.

He was a good-looking fellow, with a brown moustache, and, as they shook hands, he regarded Dr. Lyall with an air of extreme amusement.

'I hope you will excuse my costume,' observed the latter, nervously aware of this good-natured scrutiny.

'Well, do you know, I rather like it—looks Oriental and imposing. I believe I recognise that shawl pattern. How do you find yourself after your nap? Pretty fit? No bad symptoms? That's right! Well, I have brought you your things, and there's a note somewhere'—fumbling in his breast-pocket; 'let me light those candles—we can scarcely see each other—and I may as well throw on another log. Here is your note, and the ladies want to know if you will have some tea.'

'No, thanks. I have been indulging in something stronger. I am sorry you should have troubled yourself with that heavy bag.'

'No trouble at all. Besides, Rogers carried it, only he could not make you hear—you were sound asleep. I was afraid something had happened, and we should have to burst the door open. I was sorry I was not in time to be of any service; that is just my luck! I never am in time for anything. Never mind! I am delighted to find you are no worse for your cold bath, and of course'—with a slight change of tone—'we are all awfully obliged to you, and all that sort of thing, for rescuing my cousin.'

'Your cousin!' in some perplexity.

'Well, Miss Meredith is a sort of cousin; did you think she was my sister? By-the-bye, I have not introduced myself. My name is Hamlyn, and Hake is one of my chums. That reminds me that we are to dine with him presently, and it is half-past six now. What do you propose to do, Dr. Lyall? My uncle has entreated me almost with tears in his eyes to use all my powers of persuasion to keep you here to-night, and let me be the bearer of your excuses. It is an awful bore putting on one's war-paint and making one's self agreeable when one has just had a ducking, and you are tolerably snug here, eh?'

'I agree with every word you say, Mr. Hamlyn, especially with the last clause; but please make Sir Godfrey understand that I am bound to fulfil my engagement. Thanks to my hot bath and glass of stiff grog, I believe I shall escape even a cold.'

'All right; we will drive you over, then. Shall I send up someone to unpack for you?'

'Thanks awfully, but I am accustomed to be my own valet. I shall not be long over my toilet. By-the-bye, Mr. Hamlyn, I have not asked after your cousin yet. I trust she is feeling no ill effects from her accident?'

'Oh dear no; she is as fit as possible. She is actually insisting on going to the dinner-party; her mother is nearly in tears over her perversity, and my uncle is storming up and down the hall like an old lion; but they may as well spare their breath,' continued the young man dryly. 'My cousin has a will of her own.'

'Do you think it would be any use my sending a message?' asked Dr. Lyall. Such imprudence vexed his professional soul. 'I am a medical man, and I am quite sure that, after such a shock, she ought to keep perfectly quiet. Will you tell her so from me?'

'Yes, certainly; but I am afraid she will go, all the same. Now I will leave you in peace. *Au revoir!*' And as he closed the door, Dr. Lyall could hear him whistling along the passage.

'A pleasant, gentlemanly fellow,' was Dr. Lyall's inward comment as he unstrapped his Gladstone. Then a slight frown contracted his forehead. 'Is that girl mad?' he said to himself. 'There is no foolishness of which a woman is not capable. I suppose she means to put on a thin dress. Perhaps,' still more disgustedly, 'a low dress. If I were her mother I would lock her up in her room. Pamela can be unreasonable sometimes, but even she would not act in this crazy fashion. By the way, where is Pamela's note? I forgot all about it. Of course, it is in pencil, and nearly illegible.'

'Dear Alick,

'So sorry for your accident! How on earth did you get to the lake in Chesterton

Park? This is a mystery. Did you lose your way, after all? What a goose you were to get out of the carriage!

'I have sent your things. Do pray put in an appearance as soon as possible, or we shall think you are half drowned. The Hakes are in such a fuss, for fear their dinner-table should be put out. So come if you possibly can, and I will promise to nurse you, and not laugh at you more than you deserve

'Your affectionate sister,

'PAM.'

'I have almost a mind not to go, after all,' growled Dr. Lyall, seizing his hair-brushes rather fiercely. 'Put out their dinner-table indeed! Rubbish! A nice sisterly letter, upon my word! and a capital nurse she would make, too. I always told her that if I were ill she should not cross the threshold of my room. A sick man does not want a bit of quicksilver dancing attendance on him. Pam is too jerky, too original altogether, to make a comfortable nurse. If she had been in that ice-hole we should both have been drowned to a dead certainty, as sure as my name is Alexander Lyall; she could not keep still to save her life. I pity Vincent—I do from my heart. He will never tackle her properly. How can any sensible fellow tackle an anomaly?' And with these fraternal reflections Dr. Lyall continued his toilet.

He cast a look of regret round the room as he prepared to quit it. What a shame to leave that splendid fire! He would rather have liked to have occupied that comfortable-looking bed for one night. That young fellow was right; it was an awful bore turning out this cold evening, with only the prospect of having to make himself agreeable to some stranger for two hours. As a rule, he rather liked dinner-parties, but he was lazy, and not disposed to exert himself. He consoled himself, however, with the thought that he would not have to endure the monopoly of Sir Godfrey's conversation. Besides, Hake was a capital fellow, and his wife one of the nicest women possible. Why, once upon a time, he had been rather smitten with her, before Hake carried her off. If only people would hold their tongues about the unlucky accident; but, alas! it would be public property by this time.

He had not a notion where to go, but he intended to make his way to the hall. Perhaps he might find some servant there to direct him.

As he walked down the corridor he was sure he heard voices. They seemed to proceed from below. As he prepared to descend the staircase, he looked cautiously over the carved balustrades, and an unexpected sight met his eyes. The whole family seemed gathered round the hall fire. He had never seen anything more picturesque: it reminded him of a scene in a play. It was a large square hall, heavily wainscoted in oak, with two handsomely-carved screens, one of which shut out the draught of the front-door, and the other hid the staircase.

Even in that subdued light he could see that the walls were covered with trophies and weapons of every description—splendidly mounted guns and pistols, suits of rusty armour, and a bristling array of javelins, battle-axes, halberds, and daggers, while antique cabinets, full of archæological treasures, occupied the corners. An oak settle and some heavily-carved chairs were arranged in a semicircle round the fire, while tables littered with every description of feminine and masculine employment gave an air of comfort to the whole scene. He would willingly have looked a little longer, but it was impossible to remain there unperceived. He must summon up courage to join the family circle.

'Here is our guest, my dear,' he heard Sir Godfrey say, as he stepped from behind the screen. 'How do you find yourself, my dear sir?'—shaking him vigorously by the hand. 'Honoria, this is Dr. Lyall—my daughter, Mrs. Meredith;' and a pale ladylike woman rose at once with smile and outstretched hand.

'I have been longing to thank you,' she said in a pleasant voice that was very agreeable to his ear. Dr. Lyall always liked women to have soft voices. 'I have been too much engrossed with my poor child to see after your comfort myself, but I trust you had everything you wanted. It was such a terrible shock to us when Mr. Brown brought her home in his carriage! I cannot bear to think of what would have happened but for you. Doris, you must help me thank

Dr. Lyall;' and then a tall young lady, with light curly hair came up to him, whom he at once recognised as the younger sister.

'I wish we knew how to thank you properly,' she said, with frank eagerness, and there was no trace of shyness in her manner, only a gentle friendliness that took him by surprise. 'I saw it all, Dr. Lyall; I heard Gerda scream, and saw her fall,' with a shudder, 'and then you went to her and I rushed away to get help. Ah, how brave you were! No,' as Dr. Lyall muttered something in reply to this, 'of course you do not like to be thanked; but it is such a relief to us—is it not, mother?—and Gerard told me I must say something pretty.'

If he only knew how to answer this girlish outburst—if he were not such an utter fool! He could talk fluently enough on most occasions, he had strong opinions on most subjects, and had never found much difficulty in airing his views; but he was a modest man, and disliked to hear his own praises even from his patients' lips. If he had been alone with this young lady, if her blue eyes had only confronted him, he could have acquitted himself very tolerably; but there were Sir Godfrey and Mr. Hamlyn in the background, and to his relief Mr. Hamlyn came promptly to his rescue.

'Dr. Lyall quite understands, so you may as well let him warm himself before the carriage comes round; don't move, Uncle Godfrey, I will give him my corner.—By the way, Doris, you had better tell Gerda to hurry up, or we shall be late.'

A quick look of alarm crossed Sir Godfrey's countenance: its urbane expression changed to one of intense anxiety; if a bomb had suddenly exploded in the midst of the circle, he could not have seemed more visibly discomposed.

'Dear, dear, Gerard, I hope you are wrong,' he said rather nervously. 'Late? I have never been late at a dinner-party in my life. Doris,' in a quick, imperative voice, 'tell your sister from me, that if she has made up her mind to commit suicide—suicide; yes, that is the correct word—she has no right to add to her sin unpunctuality; that I shall be excessively displeased—excessively——Why, the child has gone without allowing me to finish my sentence!'

'There are two sins that my uncle regards

as unpardonable,' observed Mr. Hamlyn in an airy manner: 'unpunctuality, and killing foxes.'

'You may add a third,' returned Sir Godfrey sharply: 'want of reverence—want of reverence, Gerard. We live in sad times, Dr. Lyall; young folk nowadays know better than their elders. I was differently brought up; we were taught consideration and courtesy—consideration and courtesy. Why, when I was a young man I would as soon have thought of knocking my father down as of keeping him waiting; he was short in his temper, and would not have stood it for a moment. Of course you laugh, Gerard—you laugh at everything; all the same, I must trouble you to ring that bell.—Dalton,' as the butler entered, 'order the carriage round at once — at once. — If Gerda be not ready,' addressing his daughter, 'I regret to say we must go without her; we owe it to Dr. Lyall not to keep him any longer from his friends.'

What had come to his suave, hospitable host? There was a shade on Sir Godfrey's brow; his bland loquacity was replaced by sharp, querulous tones: could a delay of a few minutes have ruffled his equanimity so seriously, or had Mr. Hamlyn's flippant remarks given offence? He stole a glance at him. Mr. Hamlyn was arranging the flower in his buttonhole, and seemed perfectly at his ease—he even hummed something under his breath.

If Dr. Lyall had known the Hamlyn temperament, he would not have troubled himself at Sir Godfrey's quick change of mood.

The Squire's temper was by no means perfect. He had many virtues; he was truthful, kind-hearted, and made an excellent landlord. When he loved, he attached himself strongly; but he was an autocrat by nature, and somewhat narrow-minded and obstinate, and he was given to be arbitrary even in trifles. As he said himself, every man ought to be master in his own house.

Once upon a time, when Gerard Hamlyn's curly head was brimful of boyish mischief, a roughly scrawled sheet was found posted over the barometer in the hall one morning, headed:

'MY UNCLE'S BAROMETER.

'The following forecast for to-day was prepared at the Meteorological Office :

10 a.m. South-westerly winds; undulating; fair as a whole.

12 p.m. Wind decidedly in the east, becoming less mild.
2 p.m. Colder; changeable.
4 p.m. A moderate gale, strong and fresh.
6 p.m. Temperature tolerably even.
8 p.m. Look out for squalls.'

Happily, this remarkable specimen of boyish wit was promptly removed by Dalton; but it was remarked by Sir Godfrey more than once that day that the servants seemed unusually merry.

Carriage-wheels were distinctly audible, and at the same moment the younger Miss Meredith came quickly round the screen, followed by a pale, slim girl in white, who regarded Dr. Lyall with singular earnestness as she passed him, and then stopped and, half hesitatingly, put out her hand.

'I'm afraid this is hardly prudent,' he began; but she turned quickly away with a faint smile, and beckoned the maid to bring her her wraps.

'Do you know you have actually kept us five minutes waiting, Gerda?' gasped Sir Godfrey. He was just getting into his great-coat, and the exertion made him a little breathless.—'Gerard, put your cousin in the carriage; Dr. Lyall and I will follow. Now, my dear sir'—with an old-fashioned bow and dignified wave of the hand; and Dr. Lyall reluctantly preceded him.

He ensconced himself silently in his corner, and watched the gleams from the carriage-lamps flashing along the snowy road. Miss Meredith was equally silent, and made no attempt to address him. He had already decided that neither of the sisters was pretty, and he was not disposed to change this opinion. Nevertheless, competent authorities had adjudged to the elder Miss Meredith a tolerable share of good looks. She was interesting, people said, and rather uncommon-looking. She had undeniably good points—a clear, pale complexion, and hair of that soft, pretty tint of fairness that in certain lights and under certain conditions looks golden.

Dr. Lyall had noticed none of these beauties, but two things had struck him—first, the grave intentness of the look with which she had regarded him; and, secondly, the simplicity of her attire, for her white neck and arms were devoid of all ornament.

Her taciturnity repelled him, and he made no attempt to draw her into conversation.

Strange to say, though, as a rule, he disliked thanks, her total silence seemed to him misplaced and in bad taste.

'It is impossible to understand a woman,' he thought sarcastically. 'One would have expected a civil word, after a fellow has plunged up to the neck in cold water on her account. I suppose she considers me a bear for not asking how she is; but'—a little obstinately, for Dr. Lyall could be obstinate— 'I have already prescribed for her, and sent her a message, but she has refused to follow my advice.' And then he asked Sir Godfrey how far it was to Braeside.

'We shall be there directly; we turn down the next corner,' was the reply. 'Gerda my dear, you are very quiet. I have not heard your voice yet. I have been waiting to hear you make some pretty speeches to Dr. Lyall. In my time, a girl would have found something to say to the man who had just saved her life—eh, Gerard?'

'You need not ask me, sir. I am green with envy; it is just like my luck—I am never in time for anything. If you are going to make a speech, Gerda, you must hurry up.'

'One cannot make speeches to order,' returned his cousin in a cold, quiet voice.

And then the carriage stopped, and the next moment a jovial voice rang through the darkness: 'Where's Lyall? What have you done with him, Sir Godfrey? Ah, there you are, my dear fellow, large as life! Let me have a look at him, Miss Meredith, and then I will take you into the drawing-room. So you have been half drowned, old man, and are none the worse for it!' And, with a friendly clap on the shoulder, Captain Hake turned to Miss Meredith; next moment there was a confusion of hand-shaking, laughter, and sympathetic speeches, as Mrs. Hake and the assembled guests crowded round Sir Godfrey and his grand-daughter.

Dr. Lyall had greeted his hostess, and had then retreated to the hearthrug, where he was followed almost immediately by a short, dark young lady, in a yellowish silk dress, who looked at him half mischievously and half affectionately.

'Alick, what an absurd boy you have been! However could you go and do it?'

'I confess I don't see the absurdity, Pamela.'

'Well,' in a teasing voice, 'I will refrain from enlightening you, for I see that you are quaking with apprehension at the ordeal that lies before you. Do you know, Gertrude means to thank you for enlivening her dinner-party—dinner-parties are so awfully slow at Chesterton : people never know what to talk about. And now you have furnished them with conversation ; you should just have heard their tongues wagging before you came in ! Is that pale girl the heroine ? What a pity she is not prettier ! I don't care for that sort of washed-out beauty, do you know. You have to take her in to dinner ; it was all arranged beforehand, and Gertrude says it must be fate.'

'I wish you would shut up, Pam ;' and Dr. Lyall's tone was decidedly unamiable.

'Alick,' remarked his sister severely, but there was a merry little dimple belying her tone, ' I am afraid your cold bath has not improved a temper by no means naturally sweet.'

And then, as Captain Hake came towards them, she moved lightly away ; and the next moment she had the pleasure of seeing her brother standing, looking very stiff and uncomfortable, by Miss Meredith's side.

CHAPTER III.

BREAKING THE ICE.

'It is good to rub and polish our brain against that of others.'—MONTAIGNE.

DR. LYALL inwardly owned that his sister was right. He was in an execrable temper; he was tired, cold, and Pamela had, as usual, rubbed him up the wrong way. Everything was against him. He had to take in the very girl whom he was most anxious to avoid—a haughty young woman, who would not deign to acknowledge him except by a flicker of a white eyelid as she bowed in response to her host's introduction.

'No need to introduce my old friend, Dr. Lyall—eh, Miss Meredith? I'll be bound you two know each other well enough by this time; nothing like an accident for breaking the ice. Ah! ah! I call that good—never meant it, though. Just listen, Gertie; have you ever heard a better joke?' And Captain Hake moved away with his jolly laugh, and they could hear him repeating his speech to a group of admiring auditors: 'Breaking the ice—ha! ha!'

Dr. Lyall's dark eyebrows contracted more closely. He was not a tall man, but he looked so at times when he held up his head in that way and squared his shoulders; he had a sturdy, strongly-built figure that somehow suited his face.

He was by no means a handsome man, and his best friend would hardly have called him good-looking; but he looked sensible and reliable. Perhaps his mouth was his best feature—his lips closed very firmly, and his smile was frank and sweet: one of his patients said it always had the effect of sudden sunshine on her. But there was no smile on his face now, as he stood moodily pulling his moustache and staring over Miss Meredith's head. She was speaking to the lady next her, and had not thought it necessary to break off her conversation; she had a smooth, quiet voice, and he listened to it half absently.

'It has done me no harm, thank you; at least, I hope not. I am really strong, you know.'

'I should not have said so. Doris is the only strong one of the family. I am sure you are terribly imprudent to be here to-night.'

'I am afraid we must go in to dinner, Miss Meredith,' he had observed at this point. And then she had turned and put her hand in his arm. Was she shy? Did her silence proceed from diffidence? He hardly thought so, and as they seated themselves, and he handed her the menu with a commonplace remark on the beauty of the flowers before them, his bored look was plainly visible to his sister.

'Poor Alick! he is not enjoying himself a bit,' she thought compassionately; 'and no wonder, with that stick of a girl next him.' And then she addressed herself with renewed vivacity to the young barrister beside her. He was clever and amusing, and knew how to talk. Besides, he was a friend of a certain gentleman with whom she was on intimate terms.

'You know Derrick Vincent, I'm told,' he had said to her the moment they were introduced.

'Of course I do. I am engaged to him, as Mrs. Hake has probably told you,' was her quick reply. And then he had laughed, and had admitted the fact. And after that they had got on excellently together. No man with an ordinary amount of intelligence ever found it difficult to get on with Pamela Lyall.

A few more platitudes, which his companion answered in monosyllables, and then Dr. Lyall turned his attention to his soup. As he partook of it, he was wondering whether he might venture to recommend Miss Meredith to take a glass of wine. He had been struck by her paleness, and he was by no means convinced that she was as well as she made herself out to be. He had noticed an involuntary shiver, and again he told himself savagely that women, even the best of them, were fools. He was just making up his mind to run the risk of a rebuff, when he was electrified by hearing her speak to him in a quick, nervous voice:

'Dr. Lyall, what must you have thought

of me? I have been all this time in your company, and have never thanked you yet for coming to my help in that noble way. I am quite ashamed of myself. I must have seemed so cold, so ungrateful.' And then she broke off, and commenced plaiting her table-napkin into folds with her white fingers.

Dr. Lyall sat bolt upright, and motioned away some turbot with an impatient gesture, though he was particularly partial to that fish. For the moment he was almost too surprised to answer. Then he returned abruptly, but not unkindly:

'Please don't mention it; there is not the slightest occasion to trouble yourself. It is an awful bore, that sort of thing.'

This was vague, to say the least of it, and Miss Meredith looked still more disturbed.

'I am sure you are offended with me.' And her lip gave a little quiver as she spoke.

'You are wrong,' he returned warmly. 'I am not in the least offended.' A white fib that, Dr. Lyall! 'Why should you thank me? Anyone would have acted as I did under the circumstances.'

'I am not so sure of that. Some men

would have hesitated, and then it would have been too late. Of course, I know that you saved my life. I felt myself sinking, and then you caught me. Oh, it was so sudden and so terrible. Do you know,' speaking still lower, as though she were afraid she would be overheard, ' I meant to thank you. I came downstairs with that purpose, but they were all there looking at me. Of course, they were waiting to hear me say it. Do you know that feeling, when people are expecting you to do something, and you are determined to disappoint them? It was very bad of me. I am afraid I shall shock you, but I am often like that.'

He could not forbear a smile, though she was speaking almost with solemnity. But his smile was a very pleasant one. He was agreeably deceived. The haughty young woman, as he had called her, was accusing herself with the artless *naïveté* of a child. He was amused—nay, more, he was interested. An ordinary girl would not have so frankly owned herself in the wrong.

'I am afraid I have shocked you,' she continued penitently. 'Of course, a man never feels like that.'

'You are wrong there, Miss Meredith. We have our tempers, too. Now you have finished your confession, I will promise you full absolution if you will drink that glass of champagne at your elbow. I am a medical man, you know, and I think you ought to respect my advice.'

'Very well, you shall be obeyed. But I cannot eat,' as he looked meaningly at her untouched plate. 'Please go on with your own dinner; I am not hungry to-night.' And then for a little while he left her to her own devices.

But he resumed the conversation presently with a zest that surprised himself. Dr. Lyall was not a lady's man — young unmarried women often complained that he was stiff and cold in his manner to them — but the fact was, the ordinary run of girls, with their free and flippant manners, failed to please him. They were too independent and out-spoken; they had little reticence, and no reserve. He was always telling Pamela so — none of them came up to his private standard. In his eyes no woman was attractive unless she combined softness and refinement of manners with her other virtues. No doubt the girls he met on his daily rounds would make excellent wives and mothers, but he could not have fallen in love with one of them. When Vincent came to him and told him that he wanted to marry Pamela he had hardly been able to disguise his surprise. Somehow, the idea that any man would want to marry Pamela had never entered his head. Well, there was no accounting for taste; he must remember that.

Miss Meredith was leaning back in her chair, with her eyes fixed thoughtfully on the lady nearly opposite her, and he stole a quick glance at her unperceived. He thought he rather admired her style, it was so uncommon. Her head was a little bent, and the crown of fair plaits shone like gold in the lamplight. When he had seen them last, they had been unloosened, and hung heavily over his arm. Unaware of this thought that was passing through his mind, she turned to him rather quickly.

'I am wondering who that lady can be—the one in yellow silk. I have never seen her before, and I know most of the Hakes friends. Do you know her name?'

'Certainly I do. She is my sister.'

'Your sister!'

'She is my younger sister, and keeps my house—at least, she thinks she does—but her views on housekeeping are somewhat limited.'

'I am afraid you are rather satirical.'

'Not at all. I leave satire to Pamela—she is an adept in it.'

'Pamela! What a droll, old-fashioned name; but somehow I rather like it.'

'You have an uncommon name yourself, have you not, Miss Meredith?'

'I suppose I have—Gerda. It is pure Saxon, my grandfather says. He wanted my sister Doris to be called Rowena, but mother rebelled. She said Rowena was such an uncomfortable name.'

'I cannot say that I admire it.'

'No, nor I; but I like Gerda. I am so glad they did not call me Maria—after Sterne's Maria, you know. I believe grandfather proposed that. I always pity people with ugly names. I think people should be allowed to re-christen themselves when they arrive at a proper age. What a dreadful idea to be a Fanny, or a Sophia, or an Emma all one's life!'

'I think you may rest satisfied with your sponsor's choice.'

'Yes, and your sister also. How strange to think you are a doctor!'

'Where does the strangeness lie, Miss Meredith? I am very proud of my profession.'

'And rightly, too. I did not mean anything disparaging. It only seemed to me a curious coincidence that your business should be saving lives. But you have never risked your life before in doing it, have you?'

'I don't believe I risked it this afternoon.' Another white fib. 'You make too much of a slight service.'

'A slight service!'—her lip curling. 'Never mind, I will keep my gratitude to myself, for I see I am boring you. Nevertheless, I shall persist in thinking that I owe my life to you.'

'What nonsense!' but he reddened a little.

For the first time in his life he did not mind hearing his good deeds magnified. Perhaps it was her quiet voice or manner that pleased his taste.

As he gave her some grapes—they had arrived at dessert by this time, for their conversation had been interlarded with intervals of silence—he told himself, with a twinge of remorse, that he would never judge anyone so hastily again. He had been accusing her of coldness and pride; he had even told himself that she had been too high and mighty to condescend to talk to a humble doctor. How he had wronged her! She was treating him with the utmost courtesy and consideration. Her brief haughtiness had been confessed with childlike contrition; what he had taken for reserve had been a vain attempt to cloak feelings too deep for utterance. She was evidently different from other girls; she took life more gravely and earnestly. Most likely she was full of crude theories. Probably she made as many mistakes as other people, but he had never seen anyone so genuine.

'Do you live in London?' she asked him rather abruptly, but he shook his head.

'Not now, we live at Cromehurst; but that is near London, you know. I have gone in partnership with a doctor there; it seems a good opening,' rather reflectively.

'What is his name?—I know Cromehurst,' with a certain quickness that seemed natural to her.

'Dr. Brown—is he a friend of yours?' a little dubiously.

'Not a friend,' as though reproving the implied doubt; 'but I know him slightly—at least, I know his daughter Jessie.'

'Jessie Brown!' It was his turn to be surprised now.

'Yes, I have an aunt living at Cromehurst—Mrs. Glyn. Her husband—my uncle, I mean—is the Vicar of St. Jude's;' but she was checked by an exclamation from Dr. Lyall.

'I know Mrs. Glyn—Pamela has taken a great fancy to her——'

Here he was interrupted by an expressive look of the hostess round the table. He thought Miss Meredith rose a little reluctantly.

'How stupid just to break off in the most interesting part, and Aunt Clare is always so interesting to me!'

'Never mind; it shall be continued in our next,' he returned, following her to the door, and to this she had smilingly assented. Dr. Lyall felt a little giddy as he went back to his seat and helped himself to filberts; perhaps it was that tumble of his—perhaps——'I beg your pardon, what did you say?' in rather a confused voice.

'All right, my dear fellow; I only asked you to pass the bottle. Capital wine, this of Hake's! Did you try the madeira? No! Good heavens! then you have lost something. —Hake, old man, I am taking your name in vain; I am warning Dr. Lyall not to taste that vile concoction you call madeira—hand it up here, and it shall be subjected to medical test.—Now then, Lyall, fill your glass, and don't think of your neighbours;' and Mr. Hamlyn watched the process with friendly and unselfish interest.

Meanwhile Miss Meredith had followed the other ladies, and had seated herself closely by the fire, trusting that the group of animated talkers gathered on the rug might leave her in peace; but the next moment someone tapped her lightly on the arm with a fan, and, looking up, she saw Mrs. Hake and the vivacious little lady in yellow regarding her with some amusement.

'Dreaming, as usual, Gerda! but you must wake up; Miss Lyall wants to make your acquaintance, and you must be civil to her for her brother's sake.' And Mrs. Hake nodded and smiled as she left them, for a certain deaf old dowager claimed her attention.

'What a stupid speech!' observed Miss Lyall scornfully. 'Gertrude is not generally so awkward; is she not a handsome woman, Miss Meredith? Do you know, I was her bridesmaid seven years ago.'

'Seven years ago!'

'Yes, does it not sound dreadful? Oh, I feel quite old, I assure you; let me see, I was three-and-twenty last birthday, and Gertrude is six years older than I.'

'I always thought she was five-and-thirty at least.'

'No; Indian suns have faded her a little, that is all; but she is still a fine-looking woman. Nothing is more problematical than age; so many things add or detract from it—climate, weather, moods and tempers. Now, I don't consider myself a young person at all. I am quite as old as Gertrude—older, in fact; that is because she is so easy-going, and takes life as it comes, and I am a worrier by profession. By-the-bye'—as Gerda looked astonished at this outspoken speech—'I saw you looking at me at dinner; you asked Alick who I was; I read the question on your lips, though I could not hear a word. And then you glanced at me again; when people look at me like that, I am always dying with curiosity to know what they are thinking.'

'You make me feel as though I had been rude, Miss Lyall.'

'Not at all'—fanning herself energetically. 'A cat may look at a king. I believe I repaid your inquiring looks with interest. I was envying you with all my heart.'

'Envying me!' with a little staccato note of astonishment in her voice. What a very original young person Miss Lyall was, to be sure!

'Yes, you are quite the heroine of the evening. You and Alick—Alick is my brother—have been public benefactors. You have furnished us with a fruitful theme for conversation. Did you hear Captain Hake's joke? He does love making a joke. It was not really clever, but we all laughed at it. I really do think you are to be envied, Miss Meredith. Think how your experience of life has been enlarged since you buttered your toast at breakfast this morning. Things so seldom happen. One dresses and undresses, and eats and drinks, and sees one's friends, and that is all.'

'Of course, I know you are not serious. Like Captain Hake, you must be fond of a joke. No one in her senses could envy me such a disagreeable experience.'

'Don't be too sure of anyone's sanity. Most of us have a bee in our bonnet. But I declare you are turning quite pale at the mere recollection. I shall change the subject. Do you know Mr. Fenwick, the gentleman who took me in to dinner—Mr. Hengist Fenwick? He tells me he has a brother Horsa.'

'Yes, I know them both. They are very pleasant and agreeable young men. I think I like Mr. Hengist Fenwick best.'

'I am not at all surprised at that. From what he told me at dinner, his brother must be a prig. I assure you I found him most clever and amusing. Don't you adore lawyers?'

'I don't know. I have never thought about it. Mr. Fenwick is the only lawyer I know.'

'How odd! Why, I know a dozen at least. I formed that opinion a great many years ago. They are such well-read men, and know so much about human nature.'

'You might say the same of doctors.'

'Not in the same way. A doctor is always looking at the diseased side of human nature, and the idea is not wholesome. I did so want Alick to be a lawyer, but he is mad on his profession.'

'He is quite right,' returned Gerda softly. 'Next to the clerical, it is the noblest and grandest of all professions. Fancy spending one's whole life in relieving pain!'

Pamela looked at her curiously, and slightly shrugged her shoulders.

'You are an enthusiast, Miss Meredith! What a pity my brother does not hear this panegyric on his beloved profession! He does not hear these sentiments from me. I must own he does not bore or disgust me with any talk about his cases. He is too gentlemanly for that. Besides, it is not professional. But he cannot help being grave and abstracted sometimes, and then I find him poor company.'

'Your brother tells me you live at Cromehurst,' observed Gerda tentatively. She found Miss Lyall's outspoken speeches a little embarrassing. She had no wish to talk of Dr. Lyall, professionally or otherwise. 'Jessie Brown is an old acquaintance of mine.' But Pamela received this piece of intelligence rather indifferently.

'Oh, everyone knows Jessie. But I confess she does not interest me particularly. We are both great talkers, and as I never think that she says anything worth hearing, I find her rather a bore. Don't you hate people who never look beyond the surface of things?'

'I certainly do not hate Jessie. She is a very sweet-tempered, sensible girl.'

'Oh, her sweet temper was born with her. There is no merit in that. Jessie's feelings are all nicely padded by nature. Of course, I am civil to her, because her father is Alick's partner. But we have not a taste in common.

'It seems that I have chosen an unfortunate subject for discussion. I am half afraid to mention my aunt, Mrs. Glyn.'

'Mrs. Glyn!' with a sudden change of manner. 'Oh, that is quite different. There is no one I like better. And yet I have only known her a few months. We have only lived at Cromehurst since last May. She is one of the most interesting women I know. Is she really your aunt?'

'Yes, my mother's sister—her only sister. But I am afraid we do not see much of her. I am going to stay with her soon. I am very fond of her.'

'That accounts for a certain puzzled feeling that I had when I saw you first. You seemed to remind me of someone. Of course, I see now that it is Mrs. Glyn. Your colouring is very different, but you have her expression. When I paid my first visit, I remember she looked at me in the same quiet searching way, as though she were boring for hidden treasure, and hoped it would come to light presently.'

'How absurd you are!'

'Am I? When you know me better, you will find I am always absurd when I get on with people. I never talk nonsense to Jessie Brown—she would not understand it. Ah! here come the gentlemen. What a time they have been! I suppose Captain Hake has been making some more of his jokes. Alick is steering a straight course to us. Tiresome fellow! I should like to send him away.'

Gerda felt that she could hardly endorse this opinion. Miss Lyall had charmed her with her sprightliness and frankness; even her touch of sharpness, the delicate spleen that had infected some of her speeches, had only added piquancy to her talk; but she was not unwilling to admit Dr. Lyall to the conversation, and she welcomed him with the gentle smile that was habitual to her, but he had scarcely opened his mouth to make a remark, when her cousin came up to her.

'I am sorry to interrupt you, Gerda,' he said; 'but that ass Johnson has put in an appearance half an hour too soon, and now Uncle Godfrey declares that the horses are not to be kept waiting. I always said Johnson ought to have the sack; he has done it on purpose.'

'Nonsense, Gerard! he is only getting a little deaf, poor old man! But must we really go?' and there was a trace of disappointment in her tones. 'It is so early, and Mrs. Hake will think it so unkind to break up her party. Shall I speak to grandpapa?' But Mr. Hamlyn shook his head so decidedly at this, and elevated his eyebrows in such a meaning fashion, that Gerda took the hint like a wise woman, and rose at once.

'We shall be near neighbours for the next few days,' observed Dr. Lyall, as he shook hands with her, 'so I hope I shall have the pleasure of seeing you again.'

'Of course we shall see Miss Meredith,' interposed his sister in her quick way; 'she is coming to stay at St. Jude's Vicarage soon. Besides, I dare say we shall all be skating in Chesterton Park to-morrow; Gertrude was talking about it this afternoon. Of course you will be there, Miss Meredith?'

'I am quite sure Miss Meredith will do nothing of the kind,' returned Dr. Lyall decidedly. 'If she will take my advice, she will avoid the lake for a day or two,' for his quick eyes had noticed an involuntary shiver on the girl's part.

'I do not know,' was the doubtful reply. 'Doris will be there, and you must all come up to tea at the Hall;' and then she turned away and made her excuses to her hostess, and again Dr. Lyall was conscious of that slight feeling of giddiness, as he joined the group of gentlemen on the hearthrug.

CHAPTER IV.

'HE IS A DEAR, GOOD FELLOW!'

'Actions, looks, words, steps, form the alphabet by which you may spell character.'—LAVATER.

THE drive back to the Hall was happily a short one; nevertheless, Gerda leant back against the cushions and closed her eyes wearily. She was in no mood to enter into the discussion on Johnson's stupidity. At first her grandfather had assented fretfully to Gerard's wrathful remarks, and then all of a sudden he had veered round.

'I could not part with him, you know. He may be a blockhead, as you say, Gerard, but he has lived with me thirty years. I don't believe Dalton gave the order properly. A quarter to eleven, those were my words—a quarter to eleven sharp.'

'And so the carriage was brought round at a quarter-past ten. You should have sent him back, Uncle Godfrey; that would have given him a lesson. I, of course, know the horses must not stand this weather. What right has a servant to interfere with one's evening's enjoyment? I would have sent him back, and he would have been more punctual next time.'

'I dare say you would have done so,' retorted Sir Godfrey crossly. 'You young people only think of your own enjoyment. It would never enter your head that Johnson is getting old, and that sitting on the coach-box in this cutting wind is not likely to improve his rheumatism. You will learn more humanity when you are my age.'

Gerard felt inclined to retort. But he was a good-tempered fellow, and decided to hold his peace. Johnson's rheumatism was not the cause of this early break-up—he knew better than that. Sir Godfrey was tired, and had hailed the prospect of their speedy departure with rapture. He was getting old as well as Johnson, and he rather missed his evening nap. He had caught at the excuse, and would listen to no plea on his host's part. The horses could have been housed in the stables at Braeside, Johnson could have warmed his old bones in the servants' hall, and Gerda could have finished her conversation with Dr. Lyall, if only he would have listened to reason.

'I'll pension them all off when I am master,' thought Gerard for the hundredth time. 'A pack of lazy old fools!' And then he hummed a tune, and drummed on the frosted window-pane, while Sir Godfrey grumbled on.

The ladies were still in the drawing-room, Dalton informed them, so Sir Godfrey at once betook himself thither, to pour his last real or imaginary grievance into his daughter's attentive ear. As he marched across the hall, with his aristocratic old nose well in the air, Gerard whispered slily in his cousin's ear.

'Poor old boy! he is put out with me because I was hard on Johnson. Did you hear him just now: "Go home, Johnson, and have something hot. I will tell Mrs. Morgan to send you some whisky. We are getting too old to be out in this weather." I believe those two old fellows play into each other's hands. It is an understood thing between them that when the Squire goes out the carriage is to be brought round half an hour earlier than it is ordered.'

'Nonsense, Gerard! how can you talk so ridiculously?'

'Well, I won't. But—eh—what,' staring at her reproachfully, 'you are not going to leave me? Are you aware,' in an injured voice, 'that you have not spoken a word to a fellow all this evening?'

'I am quite sure that I have spoken a great many words to a fellow; indeed, I was talking to one for nearly two hours.'

'Oh, you mean Lyall! Don't try to be funny, my fair Saxon. It does not suit your style at all.'

'I am so tired that I have not a grain of fun left in me. I have a horrible disjointed feeling, as though my limbs don't belong to me. If you will keep me when I want to go to bed, you might have the courtesy to bring me a chair.'

'You are in a captious mood, I see,' as he obeyed her. And then he relented at the sight of her pale face. 'Poor little thing! I expect that tumble rather upset you. Do you know,' pulling his moustache, and looking at her plaintively, ' I owe that fellow a grudge. I would have given a good deal to have been in his place.'

In spite of her fatigue, Gerda burst out laughing.

' May I ask the reason of this unseemly mirth ?' And there was a cloud on Gerard's genial face, though he still spoke in mock wrath. ' Do you think I should not have pulled you out as quickly as he did ?'

Gerda restrained her desire to laugh again.

' Don't, Gerard, there's a good boy! Don't pretend to be jealous, or I shall be rude enough to repeat your own words, and say it does not suit your style at all.'

' I never said I was jealous,' in a decidedly aggressive voice. ' You women think such a lot of yourselves. I only said that I wished I had been in his place.'

' And it was very nice of you to say it,' soothingly. ' Don't let us quarrel, Gerard. We never do misunderstand each other, do we ?' And there was something pointed in Gerda's tone. ' Did you talk to Miss Lyall at all ? Oh, I forgot—there was no time.

She is such a droll, amusing little person; but I fancy she has a great deal in her. They live at Cromehurst, and Aunt Clare is a friend of hers. They are going to stay for the remainder of the week at Braeside, so I dare say we shall see a good deal of them.'

'Humph! I have no objection.' And Gerard spoke in his usual good-humoured tone. 'Lyall seems a pleasant fellow, and as pleasant fellows are not as plentiful as blackberries in these benighted parts, one must be thankful if one comes our way now and then.'

'Do you think he has a good practice, Gerard?'

'My dear child, how on earth am I to know Dr. Lyall's private affairs?'

'No, of course not. I only meant—how could he leave his patients for a week?'

'Oh, I see. That is easily answered. Business was slack—doctors have slack times, you know—and he had not been well, and his partner made him take a week's holiday; he told me so himself.'

'Not well!' and Gerda's face lengthened visibly.

'You are thinking the cold water was

rather bracing treatment for an invalid. Don't be afraid; a man of Dr. Lyall's sturdy build is not made of sugar or salt. Now, in spite of your bad treatment of one of the best fellows of my acquaintance, I am going to be magnanimous, and allow you to retire. Say good-night prettily and civilly, and I will light your candle;' and Gerard was as good as his word.

'He is a dear boy, and I am very fond of him!' thought Gerda, as she walked slowly up the broad staircase; but she sighed as she said this, and a troubled look came into her eyes.

The sisters' rooms had a door of communication between them; in fact, Gerda's room could only be reached by passing through Doris's. It was smaller and less convenient in many ways, but it had one advantage in Gerda's eyes—it possessed a window, small-paned and heavily mullioned, with a charming view of the park, and a glimpse of the lake shining between the trees; and this view, so green, so tranquil, was a continual feast to Gerda.

Both rooms were prettily — nay, handsomely—furnished; but the most casual eye would have noted a marked difference in all minor details. If it be true, as some wise-acres have affirmed, that a person's room is a sure exponent of his secret tastes and desires—a sweeping assertion that must be taken with a grain of salt, for frequently it is the exponent of some deceased relative's taste—these prettily-furnished virginal chambers showed a great dissimilarity in the disposition of the sisters.

Most young people would have given the preference to Doris's room—it was so neat, so charming in its arrangements, so full of girlish nick-nacks. Nothing had been omitted. A little French timepiece ticked on the mantelpiece, vases of fresh flowers were on the toilet-table, some beautifully-framed landscapes and the head of a girl adorned the faintly-stencilled walls, and a small collection of favourite poets—sacred and profane—were arranged in the tiny bookcase.

Gerda's room was equally well furnished, but there was a touch of severe simplicity in its details. There were no nick-nacks—only a single vase of flowers and some ivory brushes were on the toilet-table.

A proof engraving of 'Mors Janua Vitæ' hung opposite the bed, and two or three other fine engravings, all of sacred subjects, were carefully arranged on the wall. A carved oak cupboard and antique-looking desk, and some books in quaint, heavy bindings, were the only objects that attracted the eye.

A low easy-chair stood beside the fire-place. After a moment's hesitation Gerda sank into it — weariness prevailed against common-sense. She knew she ought to go to bed at once. Her head ached, and she felt oppressed with unusual lassitude.

'I suppose I have been a fool,' she told herself with tardy penitence, for she was never slow in acknowledging her faults to herself or others. Conscience was taking her revenge. Of course, her mother and Doris had been right, and she had been wrong. She had known all the evening that she ought to have been in her own room; and yet how she had insisted to everyone that nothing ailed her, that she was well—perfectly well. She had said as much to Dr. Lyall, and he had calmly looked her in the face, and flatly contradicted her.

'You are not well at all, and unless you rest, you will find that out for yourself to-morrow.' She had thought him very rude at the time. No gentleman, not even a doctor, should contradict a lady; but she was obliged to own now that he was a true prophet. Why had she been such a self-willed goose, and given them all so much trouble? Her mother had almost shed tears over her wilfulness. She had acted in a way that surprised herself, for she had even shown temper to Dr. Lyall. What had made her so anxious to go to this special dinner-party—she, who always voted dinner-parties as altogether ridiculous for young people? Well, her motives had been somewhat mixed, and, in short, she was too tired to try and analyze them. She had been anxious to thank the man who had saved her life. She had even felt some degree of curiosity about him; he had been kind; yes, on the whole, his conversation had interested her, and she had been sorry when it had been interrupted; but, all the same, she was not sure she liked him. He had such a quiet manner—almost a repressive manner. It had kept her in check, somehow. Her gratitude — her very natural gratitude—had seemed to embarrass him. She had never seen a man so put out of countenance by a few simple remarks. He must be rather reserved—a self-contained, modest sort of person—and yet he looked very clever. Now and then he seemed as though he were laughing at her—yes, she was sure he was satirical. When he knew a person well, he would say teasing things; and yet once or twice there had been something gentle, almost sympathetic, in his tone.

'He has a firm mouth—of course, a doctor ought to be firm, or his patients would not trust him. I wonder why I can't make up my mind if I like him or not. I generally either like or dislike a person at once.' She paused, stifled a yawn, and then muttered under her breath, 'Most decidedly I do not dislike him—on the contrary, I should rather like to talk to him again.'

'You naughty child!' observed a crisp young voice from the outer room. 'Do you know you have never bidden mother good-night? Gerard came in just now and said you had gone to bed. We thought you were chattering to him in the hall. Why'

—and here Doris appeared in the doorway—'you have not even taken off your dress yet.'

'I was too tired to move. I forgot mother—shall I go down to her now?'

'For pity's sake, no!—your white face would give her a nightmare. Besides, Grand is talking to her, and he is not exactly in a nice mood. They have got on the old subject; that's why I ran away. Oh dear'—as Gerda shivered—'you are cold! Do make haste, for your bed is so nice and warm. Shall I brush your hair?—you are not a bit fit to do it yourself;' and to this Gerda languidly assented.

'It is so funny!' she said drowsily, as Doris skilfully manipulated the long fair hair that almost enveloped her; 'I am as tired as possible, and yet I do not feel sleepy. How nicely you brush, Dorrie—so smoothly and quietly! You have no idea how soothing it is when one's head aches.'

'Have you got a headache, poor dear?' in a delightfully sympathetic voice. 'I am so sorry; I wanted to talk to you about the dinner-party. Gerard said Dr. Lyall took you in to dinner—but I suppose I must not ask any questions; it will only make your head worse.'

'I do not mind talking if you will only go on brushing. Yes, Dr. Lyall took me in to dinner, and we had a long talk. Is it not strange—he lives at Cromehurst, and they actually know Aunt Clare! When we went into the drawing-room Mrs. Hake introduced his sister to me.'

'Is she nice?'

'Yes, I think so; but she is very original. I never heard anyone talk in quite the same way; but I found her very interesting.'

'Is she pretty?'

'Well, not exactly. I thought so at dinner—she sat nearly opposite to me—and I was very much struck with her, and asked Dr. Lyall if he knew her name: he was so amused. She is little and dark; and when she talks and laughs a beautiful colour comes into her face, and makes her look so brilliant; but she is not a bit pretty really, it is only her colouring and animation. Her nose is rather aggressively pointed and obstinate looking, and her lips are too thin and close too firmly for a girl. But I must own she has bewildering eyes.'

'Dear me, Gerda! what a description! I have never seen a pair of bewildering eyes in my life.'

'I think I mean eyes that puzzle you a little, and set you wondering about their owner. Miss Lyall's eyes never looked the same for long together. One minute they were sparkling with fun and animation, and the next they had a wistful, melancholy look in them. They had always that expression when she was silent.'

'I mean to make her acquaintance to-morrow. She has evidently bewitched you—you so seldom seem interested in people. You don't tell me how you liked Dr. Lyall. I cannot say he made much impression on me, but, then, I only saw him for ten minutes. I don't like a rough brown moustache.'

'A rough brown moustache!' in rather a surprised tone.

'Yes; Dr. Lyall seems by no means particular about his personal appearance. And he looked so small and insignificant beside Gerard. Gerard was handsomer than ever this evening.'

'So you always say. I believe you are half in love with him yourself. Oh! you hurt me then. Did you pull my hair to punish me for my naughty speech? I was only in fun, Doris. You need not turn so red—I can see your reflection in the looking-glass, and you are the colour of a peony!'

'I shall leave off brushing your hair if you make such disagreeable remarks;' and Doris walked away in girlish dudgeon, but Gerda caught her by the dress.

'You silly child, to mind my absurd joke! Give me a kiss directly, and I will promise never to do it again. Come and sit down for a moment—I must ask one question. What was Grand talking about when you left the drawing-room?'

'Do you really want to know?'—rather reluctantly.

'Yes—yes—please tell me as quickly as possible.'

'Well, he told mother that he was getting sick and tired of all this procrastination, and that he meant to have a serious talk with Gerard on the first opportunity.'

'Oh dear! oh dear!'

'He said he did not believe it was Gerard's fault at all—that you were simply playing with him out of girlish perversity and nonsense; that all this stand-offishness on your part meant nothing but temper; and that mother ought to scold you into reason.'

'I don't fancy mother will try that plan,' was the dry response.

'No, poor mother looked so worried. Really, Grand gives her no peace! Should you not hate to be in her position?—she is so utterly dependent on him.'

'Not more dependent than you or I, Doris.'

'True; but, then, we are young, and have a hundred ways of amusing ourselves; we are not always at his beck and call as mother is. When anything goes wrong she always has to bear the brunt of it. It is Honoria this and Honoria that from morning to night. If I were mother, I should hate the sound of my own name.'

'Poor dear mother! she is terribly afraid of him. If only she had Aunt Clare's spirit!'

'I don't agree with you. I dare say Aunt Clare repents of having her own way. I don't believe Uncle Horace makes her really happy. I am quite sure by this time that she has repented marrying for love.'

'I shall tell her what you say one day.'

Then Doris made a little face at her sister.

'She will be dreadfully shocked, and preach sentiment for an hour on end, from sheer sense of duty. Ah, Dorrie, what a stupid world this is! What business has Grand to tyrannize over us in this medieval fashion, and insist on our being in love with each other? Such nonsense! when we have known each other from babyhood.'

'I don't see that makes any difference. Gerard is really very fond of you.'

'So am I of him. He is a dear, good fellow; I know no one better. He ought to marry the best woman in the world.'

'That is exactly what he means to do;' and Doris gave her a loving little hug.

'No, dear,' rather solemnly; 'but, all the same, I have no wish to undervalue myself. And I think I deserve more than Gerard is ever likely to offer me.'

'Why, you would be mistress of the Hall, Gerda!'—opening her eyes rather widely at this. 'The future Lady Hamlyn would be a rich woman—immensely rich!'

'What nonsense! As though I were thinking of anything so sublunary! That is your great fault, Doris: you are so dreadfully matter-of-fact. I love the dear old Hall, but, all the same, it does not follow that I should marry its master. Don't you see, goosie, we are neither of us in love with each other. Sometimes Gerard tries to make me believe that he is, but it is only pretence, and, with all his efforts, the poor boy does not do it well. There, I have worked myself up, and made my head worse! Please don't talk to me any more. If Grand is in his second childhood, I have just cut my wisdom teeth — so friends and relatives may beware of me.' And with these oracular words Gerda patted her sister on the shoulder in a patronizing fashion, and entreated to be left alone.

'There will be an awful tussle one day, and then I shall have to go to Aunt Clare,' she said to herself as she laid her head on the pillow and closed her aching eyes; but it was a long time before she could sleep. Once, just as she was dropping off into a doze, she seemed to hear the sudden crack of the ice, and felt herself sinking in the cold water, and roused up with a shudder, to find a displaced log had fallen noisily on the hearth, and that the old grandfather's clock in the hall was striking two.

CHAPTER V.

A PAGE OUT OF THE HAMLYN RECORDS.

'Men study women as they study the barometer; but they do not understand until the day after.'—*Thoughts of a Queen.*

GERDA awoke in a beautiful frame of mind the next morning. To be sure, her head still ached, but there were no bad symptoms. She was neither feverish nor shivering; no rheumatic pains racked her young limbs, and only a pleasing sense of languor induced her to yield to Doris's entreaties to lie still and take her breakfast in bed.

She was generally restive in such matters, and inclined to resist all such advice. She had a youthful dislike to any form of coddling. Mrs. Meredith was a woman who loved to exercise her maternal surveillance in season and out of season. A cold, a headache, even a finger-ache, would furnish her with an excuse for a little extra petting. It must be confessed that Gerda received those attentions somewhat impatiently, and was much given to keeping her ailments to herself.

'Don't let mother trouble to come up and see me,' had been her parting charge to Doris, and Doris had nodded an assent. Nevertheless, an hour had not passed before Gerda heard her mother's voice at the door asking for admittance.

'Were you asleep, dear? Have I disturbed you?'—kissing her. 'How shockingly pale you look! Doris says you have a headache. I think I shall ask Dr. Reynolds to look in after luncheon.'

'My dear mother,' and Gerda's placidity vanished in a moment, 'what an absurd idea! What do I want with Dr. Reynolds? I am quite well, and only a little lazy, so Doris begged me to rest. Of course, if you talk to me in this fashion, I shall have to get up at once, to prove to you that I am all right.'

'You will do nothing of the kind. What a troublesome child you are, Gerda! Well, we will not talk about Dr. Reynolds just now. I had a bad night myself. And no wonder, after all that fright and worry. And then, just because I felt as though I could bear nothing more, your grandfather kept me talking until nearly midnight.'

Gerda winced, and grew hot. She knew what was coming. Mrs. Meredith, in spite of many excellent qualities, was wholly without tact. It was by no means her habit to keep her troubles to herself. Her father gave her a great deal to bear, and she indemnified herself for her forbearance and patience to the old man by much bemoaning of her hard fate to her young daughters. And it must be owned she generally received from them a vast amount of sympathy. The girls had long ago made up their minds that their mother was kept in undue subjection. 'Grand is always so hard on poor mother,' they would say to each other. And Gerda, who had plenty of courage, would sometimes tell her grandfather so to his face.

Mrs. Meredith was a delicate-looking woman, with a soft voice and subdued manner. Her spirit had never been a high one, and her many troubles had effectually quenched it.

In her young womanhood she had been exceedingly pretty—far prettier than either of her daughters, as Sir Godfrey was often pleased to tell them; but no one would have guessed this fact from looking at her faded, gentle face.

His elder daughter had been Sir Godfrey's favourite. She had been a handsome, strong-willed girl, and she had showed her determination in persisting in marrying a poor curate, who had had the audacity to fall in love with her; and great and unappeasable had been Sir Godfrey's wrath and grief at this shameful mésalliance, as he termed it.

The Chesterton estates were strictly entailed, and Sir Godfrey's only brother, Captain Hamlyn, was his heir. Sir Godfrey's wife, a woman of good birth, had brought him little or no money, so her daughters were wholly dependent on their father's goodwill, and Clarice—or Clare, as she was commonly called—soon found herself practically disinherited.

For some years no invitation had been extended to her or her husband, and though Captain Hamlyn had at last interfered in a good-natured way, and had brought about a reconciliation, Clare had never felt herself to be forgiven.

Her visits to the Hall were few and far between, and, with the exception of his first formal acceptance of his father-in-law's hospitality, it was noticed that the Rev. Horace Glyn never accompanied his wife.

He was a proud, hard-tempered man, and he would eat no bread offered to him in such a grudging fashion.

'Honoria always says that father will come round one day,' his wife would say to him.

She thought, for their children's sake, that the old man should be humoured, but Mr. Glyn could tolerate no such feminine sophistry.

'You may go as often as you like, my dear,' he would answer coldly; 'indeed, it is your duty to do so from time to time, especially as your father is growing old. But you must excuse me if I remind you that it is no duty of mine.'

'Not for Walter's sake?' she had once added rather pleadingly, for her boy was as the apple of her eye; and then he had turned upon her almost savagely.

'No, not for Walter's sake,' he had replied. 'I suppose our children are as dear to me as they are to you, but not even to benefit them will I crawl into a man's house when I know that he hates me, and grudges me every mouthful that I eat under his roof;' and after this she had dared to say no more.

Poor Clare! she was a high-spirited woman, but she had found her master; and though she loved her husband with the intensity and tenacity of a strong nature, it may be doubted whether he made her perfectly happy.

Horace Glyn was ascetic both by habit and conviction. He was a man who on principle would have denied himself any unnecessary luxury, even if he could have afforded it; but straitened means had for many years debarred him even from the ordinary comforts.

Since then the living of St. Jude's had been offered him, and though it was by no means a very lucrative piece of preferment, it had lifted him out of the mire of poverty; and, after his own stern fashion, he had rejoiced and owned himself thankful. But his rejoicings had been feeble compared to his wife's boundless gratitude.

Clare had gallantly struggled through their season of poverty. Her love for her husband had prevented her from adding to his burdens by any undue repinings, but those years had told upon her. She had suffered, and her pride had suffered; but she had kept her trouble to herself. In later years she had unbosomed herself to her niece Gerda. A warm attachment had grown up between them, and Clare had tasted a new pleasure in Gerda's sympathy.

To her she would speak of her love for her old home, of her affection for every familiar spot. 'Honoria never cared for these things as much as I did,' she would say with a sigh, as she recalled some mossy hollow in the park, where the first violets blossomed, or the bank where they found daffodils, all a-blowing and a-growing, one March afternoon. There were other confidences between the aunt and niece—feminine confidences, that would have shocked the austere soul of Horace Glyn. Clare would confess, with much compunction, that the old Adam was as strong as ever within her—that years of poverty had not quenched her love of softness and pretty things. Gerda soon found out why her dearly-loved aunt came so seldom to the Hall.

'I should only put you all to shame with my shabby gowns and home-trimmed bonnets,' she said, with a little laugh. 'Here it does not matter. A Vicar's wife may always look shabby, and no one blames her. They only think it sets a good example. Horace would hate to see me too well dressed. He would read texts to me out of Timothy. If I want a new dress I often go without one, because I am so afraid of vexing him. He never can understand how quickly women's clothes wear out, especially now dress materials are so cheap.'

'I call it a shame of Uncle Horace,' Gerda replied, with youthful passion and vexation in her voice—for she was by no means over-fond of her stern uncle. 'You are such a good-looking woman, Aunt Clare, and when you are well dressed no one can look nicer. He ought to be proud of you, instead of begrudging you a few yards of stuff.'

'Your Uncle Horace is proud of me after his own fashion,' replied Mrs. Glyn, with a soft, peculiar smile. 'And he treats me better than he treats himself. He does not understand how much these things are to a

woman. A shabby coat or an old hat—
—aren't old hats odious, Gerda?—do not
give him an instant's pain. It is our small
minds, my dear, that inflict these minor
miseries on us. I believe in his heart he is
disappointed that I do not grow up to his
perfections. He would like me to be as
indifferent to these things as he is himself.'

'But that is impossible. Surely Uncle
Horace remembers the beautiful home from
which he took you, and that your surround-
ings were utterly different from his. He
has always had such a hard life. You have
told me so. But you have been accustomed
to luxury, and to all manner of comfort from
your babyhood.'

'Of course he remembers it. But he
thinks it ought to be banished from my
recollection. "When you did me the honour
of marrying me," he has said more than once
to me, "you knew you were to be a poor
man's wife. You gave up a great deal for
me, and I believe I am not ungrateful for
the sacrifice. But it is too late now to
regret the flesh-pots of Egypt." Was not
that speech enough to crush one?'

'Never mind,' returned Gerda, kissing her

eagerly. 'In spite of his hard speeches, Uncle Horace thinks there is no one like you.' And in this opinion Gerda's girlish shrewdness was not at fault. 'He thinks it his duty to make that sort of speech. You must come to the Hall, Aunt Clare. Who minds whether your gowns are shabby or not? I wish mamma had more money, and then she would buy you some. But Grand always looks into the accounts. If we have too many new dresses he grumbles, and says we shall ruin him.'

Gerda's remark might appear strange to anyone who was not conversant with the family history. But it was not the least part of Mrs. Meredith's troubles that she and her girls were so dependent on Sir Godfrey. Owing to some flaw in her marriage settlement — some culpable oversight on the lawyer's part—the greater part of her modest dowry had been squandered by her husband during their brief married life.

Honoria had married with her father's approval. She had been more fortunate than her sister, and had been able to gratify her inclinations without hindrance or contradiction from her natural guardian, and for a short time things had gone smoothly with the young couple.

Algernon Meredith had very little money of his own, but he was well connected, and his chief recommendation in Sir Godfrey's eyes was that he was the heir of his uncle, Lord Galveston, a peer much noted among his fellows for his eccentricity and his brief, telling speeches in the House. Great was Sir Godfrey's consternation when the news reached his ears that this worthy nobleman, already showing signs of dotage and senility —in reality he was a hale, vigorous man of sixty-two—was on the eve of marriage with a young American beauty, whose sprightly charms had captivated his elderly fancy.

For a long time Sir Godfrey refused to credit these tidings. But it soon proved no rumour, and before another year had passed Lady Galveston had given birth to a fine boy, and all chance of Algernon's succession to his uncle's title and estates was rendered null and void.

The young Captain of Hussars took his disappointment lightly. He was an easy-going fellow, and was accustomed to take life as it came. If he were a scapegrace, he was a lovable scapegrace, and was no man's enemy but his own.

The luck was dead against him, that was all; but, as he pointed out to his wife, it was now his father-in-law's duty to maintain them. Chesterton Hall was quite as comfortable quarters as Galveston Castle—in fact, of the two, he rather preferred the former; and though Sir Godfrey could not be brought to regard the matter in the same light, he nevertheless tolerated his son-in-law's society with less grumbling than might have been expected under the circumstances.

How long his patience would have lasted is extremely doubtful, but before Doris was a year old, Algernon Meredith's life terminated abruptly. He had entered some races as gentleman jockey, and was brought home a corpse. At the last hurdle his horse had fallen with him, and he had broken his neck.

Poor Honoria had mourned for him long and faithfully. With all his faults and follies, he had been an affectionate husband to her, and, woman-like, she had shut her eyes to his defects of character.

After his own fashion, her father attempted to console her. He made much of her and the children, and was never weary of pointing out that it was her duty to rouse herself for the sake of her baby-girls.

In spite of a good heart, Sir Godfrey was an autocrat even then. He begrudged his daughter no comfort. He was lavish in his gifts to her, but he expected her to conform to all his opinions and caprices.

Sir Godfrey hated the outward garb of mourning, and the sight of prolonged grief made him impatient. To please him, Mrs. Meredith soon laid aside her widow's weeds; and though she did not cease to weep for her young husband, she at least took care that her tears should be shed in secret. On only one point she ventured to oppose him. A few years afterwards he proposed that she should marry again. He had found an excellent match for her—their neighbour, a wealthy bachelor, had made overtures for the hand of the young widow. Even a worm will turn, and Honoria's womanly indignation at this proposal silenced Sir Godfrey at once and for ever.

'Pooh, pooh, my dear!' he said fretfully,

as she had finished her remonstrance with a fit of passionate crying; 'you are talking nonsense. Young widows marry again every day, and no one blames them; indeed, St. Paul recommended them to do so—you may read that for yourself. Poor Algy was the last man to wish you to go on making yourself miserable for his sake; and, after all, he was not such a loss, poor fellow! Remember, he gambled away your money.'

'Do not speak to me of his faults, father. I will not hear it, even from you;' and Honoria's eyes flashed so fiercely through her tears that Sir Godfrey drew back in alarm. Was her grief turning her brain? Then she melted, and caught her little Doris to her breast. 'What does it matter what he did with my money? He was my husband, and I begrudged him nothing— nothing! Father, you do not mean to be unkind, but you do not understand. I am Algy's widow, and I will remain so. When you are tired of me and the children, you must send us away, and I will work for them and myself too.'

'Tut, tut, don't talk nonsense!' was all his answer; but there had been a glistening in his cold blue eyes, and his voice was a trifle husky.

Honoria noticed that her father treated her with a good deal of consideration for a long time after this conversation; perhaps in his heart he respected her all the more for her fealty and devotion to the dead. Certainly, he never again alluded to a second marriage.

Sir Godfrey had had his troubles too. His only brother had died a very few years after his marriage, leaving his widow and one child, a baby, to his fraternal care. Clare and Honoria were children then, and their cousin, the elder Gerard, had been their favourite playmate at Chesterton Hall.

But the same fatality overtook him, just as he was in the prime of youth and happiness. He was attacked by some malarious fever in an Indian village, where he and two or three other officers were camping out, and he died without even having seen the child to whom his wife had just given birth.

Sir Godfrey had loved his nephew dearly; but before many years were over he had transferred his affections to the younger Gerard, and after his mother's death he had sent for the boy to the Hall, and had treated him as his own son. When the girls grew up, a new idea occurred to him—what a good thing it would be if Gerard and Gerda were to take a fancy to each other!

Gerard would have the estate; but Honoria and her children still needed provision. Sir Godfrey's fortune was only moderate — to settle his daughter comfortably in the dower-house, and provide handsomely for his grand-daughters would certainly impoverish his resources—and yet he was desirous of doing his duty to his own flesh and blood. To be sure, as conscience whispered, Clare was his own flesh and blood too, and his first-born as well; but he would not listen to this sugges-tion. 'Clare has made her bed, and must lie in it,' he thought; 'she must reap the wages of disobedience. No money of mine shall go into Horace Glyn's pocket; Honoria has always been dutiful—I must certainly provide for her and her children.'

Gerard had just finished his Oxford career, and had taken a satisfactory degree, to his own unmitigated astonishment, when this pet scheme that had been simmering in his great-uncle's brain was duly laid before him.

Gerard, who was easy-going by nature, showed no repugnance to the plan. He was fond of his cousin Gerda. She was not especially pretty; but he thought her clever and amusing, and they had always been great chums. As he was not in love with anyone else, and his uncle's arguments appeared conclusive, he was soon brought to say that, if Gerda would have him, he had no objection to marry her.

'She will have you, my boy!' returned Sir Godfrey rather hilariously, as he clapped his heir on the shoulder. 'What can she find against you—a fine-built, athletic fellow like you, who will treat her kindly, and give her her own way? Try her, Gerard—both the girls are young, and have never had a lover —it is first come, first served, in most cases; and I expect it will be so in hers.'

Gerard was not quite so sure of this. He knew enough of girls already to make him a little doubtful of results. Gerda was not the girl to say 'Yes' unless she was quite sure of herself. She would demand a good deal from the man whom she accepted as her husband; but he had pledged his word to Sir Godfrey, and one fine spring evening, as he was rowing her on the lake in Chesterton Park, he seized his opportunity and spoke to her.

It was evident that he had taken her completely by surprise; for as he looked at her, he saw that she turned very pale. She was silent for full five minutes, and he was still leaning on his oars watching her, when she glanced up at him rather sharply.

'This is not your own idea, Gerard; somebody has put this into your head.'

'My dear girl!'—in rather an offended voice.

'Oh, please don't speak in that injured tone! Of course, I am not answering you properly——' And here Gerda broke into a nervous little laugh that made Gerard feel still more uncomfortable. He had quite worked himself by his eloquence to believe he really wished this thing, and his cousin's manner did not altogether please him: 'Do be good, Gerard, and tell me who first suggested this. Was it Grand, or '—knitting her brows thoughtfully—' but, no, it could not be mother?'

'Why should it be anyone? Upon my word, Gerda, you are treating a fellow very badly! I dare say I have been a bit abrupt, and that you are not quite prepared for this; but if you will think over it quietly, and give me your answer later on, I won't press or hurry you. You may not think much of me'—with a touch of real feeling in his voice that made Gerda blush—'but I am awfully fond of you, and I am sure I should make you a good husband.'

'I am sure you would.' And here Gerda raised her eyes and looked at him contemplatively, as though she were trying to picture him in that character. 'Thank you, Gerard dear! You have done that very nicely, and it almost sounded as though you meant it; but'—suddenly beaming at him with a smile—'you and I know better than that. Have we not been just like brother and sister all our lives? We will not go and spoil everything just because Grand has got this foolish idea in his dear old head.'

'Do you mean you won't try to like me?' And Gerard's tone was as persuasive as though his whole life's happiness were dependent on her answer. He was a man, and he did not like to be beaten.

'I do like you—I love you dearly, Gerard;

but I am not going to cheat you into the belief that it is the sort of love you are asking. Put this ridiculous idea out of your head. We never shall care for each other in that way.'

'I am not so sure of that'—for her opposition put him on his mettle. In reality, he was secretly relieved at her decision; he did not care about being engaged just then; the whole thing bored him. He wanted to go and hunt bison over the American prairies with some friends of his who were just starting. He would rather eat buffalo-hump with his comrades than make love to the best and prettiest girl in the world. Nevertheless, he could not refrain from a last word.

'I will have another try, and you can just think it over,' he had said. as he took up the oars again.

But to this she had made no reply. She had given him her opinion firmly and kindly. If he chose to spoil things, and put their comfortable friendship on an uneasy footing, that was his fault, not hers.

Sir Godfrey was much chagrined when Gerard informed him of his failure; but he cheered up when the young man avowed his intention of making another attempt.

'That is right, my boy!—faint heart ne'er won fair lady. There is nothing like sticking to a woman, and letting her see that you mean it. Go away for a few months, and shoot as many buffaloes as you can; and then, when you come back, tackle her boldly—very likely she'll give you a different answer.'

So Gerard took his departure gaily, and shot his big game, and sat over his camp-fires, singing choruses to his companions' songs, and enjoyed his life with the zest of an honest, light-hearted young Englishman.

But, with all his fun, he did not forget his cousin; and even in Canada and New York, where he danced with many beautiful girls, and made love to them in his easy-going, lazy way, he never really lost his heart to one of them. He was in no hurry to go back to Gerda; he did not find absence from her at all irksome or wearisome; neither did he treasure her few letters with a lover's care. But when he saw her again, and she came to meet him with the gentle, affectionate smile with which she always greeted her favourites, he was dimly conscious that she was more interesting to him than other girls, and that it was a comfortable sort of thing to be talking to her again.

He had been back at the Hall nearly two months now; but up to this time he had not tried again, in spite of sundry strong hints and not a little grumbling on Sir Godfrey's part. And Gerda was beginning to hope that the troublesome question would not be put to her a second time.

CHAPTER VI.

'IT SHALL BE NOBODY.'

'To struggle against friends true courage is required. It is like putting out your fire to remain in the cold.'—*Thoughts of a Queen.*

WHEN Gerda heard her mother's meaning tone she moved restlessly under her eiderdown. Why had she allowed herself to be taken at this disadvantage? she thought, with an inward groan. Why had she been weak enough to yield to Doris's persuasions to lie still and rest? Of what avail such rest, if she were compelled to listen to her mother's arguments?

A certain expression on Mrs. Meredith's face, an ominous droop of the mouth, and the little nervous cough that prefaced her remarks, warned her of the gravity of the situation.

'When there is anything on one's mind it is always best to talk it all out,' as Mrs. Meredith had once observed; to which Gerda had replied dryly: 'No doubt it is highly desirable to shift one's burdens on other people's shoulders; for it is not always possible,' she went on, with youthful sententiousness, 'to ease one's mind unless the weight be deposited on your neighbour's.' For, with all her dutifulness, Gerda could be a little sarcastic at times.

Mrs. Meredith had her knitting in her hands—she was an industrious woman, and never wasted time. As she began to speak her needles moved rapidly. Somehow, that clicking accompaniment added to Gerda's inward irritation.

'Your grandfather talked to me very seriously last night, Gerda,' she began, not looking at her daughter as she spoke. 'Something must have put him out, for he seemed very fidgety. He began about Johnson, and then all at once he veered round to the old subject. Somehow, he seems to think that it is all my fault that you and Gerard have failed to come to an understanding.'

'I hope you told Grand to mind his own business?'

'Indeed, I did nothing of the kind'—knitting still more rapidly. 'How could you think that I could answer your grandfather after such a fashion! You ought to be too well aware of our position by this time. Do you want him to remind us that we owe him the very bread we eat?'

'Oh, I am quite sure that he will remind us of that!'

'Do you think that it can be pleasant to listen to such speeches, Gerda? to be told continually that I and my children are burdens? that except for his bounty we should be paupers? For your sakes I have borne a good deal; but last night I felt as though the weight of it all were too heavy for me.'

'Poor mother! It is dreadfully hard on you. He has no right to make you feel your dependent position. It is cruel and unfeeling.'

'He does not mean to be cruel; in reality, he is as fond of you and Doris as though you were his own children. He is an old man, Gerda, and old men are crotchety sometimes. He told me last night, with tears in his eyes, that his heart was set on this match, and that he wished it for both your sakes. "You must talk to her," he said more than once. "You are her mother, and ought to have influence with her; make the child see that she cannot do better for herself. There is not a finer young fellow to be found in England. As lads go, he is sound and honest to the core."'

'So he is. Grand was quite right there.'

Mrs. Meredith's face brightened. She had not expected this ready acquiescence.

'I am sure there are very few young men as good as Gerard. He has the sweetest temper in the world; and then he is so fond of you. Don't shake your head, Gerda! He told your grandfather the other night, as seriously as possible, that, as far as he was concerned, he was ready and willing to marry you to-morrow.'

A sudden flush crossed Gerda's face.

'I am very much obliged to him,' she observed resentfully; 'but in a question of marriage there are two people to be considered.'

'Yes, dear'—in a soothing voice—'I am

quite aware of that; but when Gerard spoke to you, you were taken by surprise, and it was natural that you should not be ready with the answer that he wished; but now you have had time to think it over, and really Gerard himself has so improved!'

'Mother,' interrupting her impatiently, 'what is the use of saying all this? Grand will have to give up this ridiculous project: I shall never marry Gerard—never! I know myself and him far too well to make such a mistake. If he speaks to me again, I shall tell him so plainly, and then very likely he will quarrel with me—oh, dear, how sad that will be!—but I shall not be able to help myself. Men are such odd, contradictory creatures! They want you to believe all that they choose to tell you. Gerard is not a bit in love with me, but he has got it into his head that we are to marry each other; and if I say, "No, thank you," he will be as offended as possible.'

'Oh, Gerda!' And at her mother's horrified voice Gerda's sharp tones softened.

'Poor dear mother! I forgot that you would be a sufferer too. What a temper Grand will be in when Gerard tells him! I expect that I shall have to take refuge with Aunt Clare, for I shall be sent to Coventry. To be sure, Grand cannot lock me up in my room, or condemn me to bread and water; but all the same, our meals will be terrible. You and Doris will not dare to open your lips to me in his presence, and I shall have to be grateful if Dalton does not forget to hand me the vegetables.'

'It is no laughing matter, I assure you, Gerda,' returned her mother dismally; 'and if I believed you I should be wretched at the prospect before us; but you are only a girl, and will change your mind. If you cared for anyone else, of course, it would be different; but neither you nor Doris have seen anyone.'

'You mean it must be Gerard or Nobody? Then in that case it shall be Nobody. Thank you, mother dear, for putting the matter so clearly before me. After all, I am not sure that it is a blessing to be born a girl; the men have much the best of it. If Gerard be angry with me he can go and console himself with a hundred delightful girls; but for poor unlucky me there is only Nobody.'

'Gerda, I do wish you would not talk so absurdly!'

'On the contrary, I think I am talking very sensibly, and you must allow that I did not begin the subject. After all, marrying need not be the sole end and aim of a girl's life. I know most people think so, but I choose to differ from them, and I should not be a bit surprised if I and Nobody have a tolerably pleasant life of it.'

'I think I had better go down to Doris.' Mrs. Meredith's voice was a little injured; but the spirit of mischief had taken possession of Gerda.

'After all, I am glad to know my fate,' she continued smoothly. 'I think I am rather to be envied. Think how delightful it will be to please Nobody—to expect Nobody—to quarrel with Nobody! I wonder what Gerard will think of his rival? There is no fear of them coming to blows.'

But Mrs. Meredith made no reply to this girlish jest. She only sighed once—a weary, oppressed sigh—as she closed the door. It was not the first time Gerda had proved too much for her. There were contradictions in the girl's nature that baffled her. She loved both her children dearly, but there were more points of sympathy between her and Doris. Doris's character was simpler and less complex; she was less clever than Gerda, and she made fewer demands on human nature. Doris cared for most people; Gerda admitted only a favoured few into her confidence; her fastidiousness was hard to please, and she saw faults where Doris only saw virtues. This reserve, and a secret craving to find perfection, imposed limits to her enjoyment, and prepared the way for inevitable disappointment. It is always a mistake to ask too much from one's fellow-creatures. There are flaws and defects in the noblest natures; imperfections and deficiencies—the taint and blemish of original sin—meet one at every turn; it is wiser to make allowances, to be less clear-sighted as to our neighbours' shortcomings. Gerda was guilty of this grievous error of judgment; her own aims were lofty, and she was too ready to condemn others who were satisfied with a lower plane of thought and action. She was not content to try and live up to her own ideal, but she insisted that others should do the same.

She had driven her mother away with a girlish jest, but as soon as she was left alone her mood changed. As she dressed, she questioned herself somewhat sadly. From a child Gerda had been subject to sudden fits of gravity. She would relapse into strange silent moods, of which she could give no adequate account. Once, when a mere infant, her mother had found her sitting in a corner, with her tiny hands clasped over her eyes.

'Don't 'peak to me, mammie; I am having a big fink,' she observed solemnly; and this precocious speech had been treasured in the mother's memory, and had become a family joke.

Gerda felt herself on the edge of a 'big think' now, as she stood looking out on the low gray skies and the bare branches of the elms. The sombre, wintry prospect outside her warm room seemed to frame her thoughts fitly. Her mother's words had imparted a touch of frost to the moral atmosphere round her—a chill breath of impending trial, of sudden dilemma, filled her with foreboding. What had she done to bring this trouble on herself? — for in her secret soul she owned it a trouble. Hitherto things had been smooth with her; if her life had been uneventful and a trifle monotonous, it had presented no difficulties; there was no dissonance in her environment; certain phases of youthful discontent that had been habitual to her had only been like the rising of healthy sap in some vigorous tree—a sign of life and growth—for even discontent may prove nobility of nature.

'With all my faults I have always been true to myself,' she thought, with a sudden bitter presentiment — that holding to the truth under certain conditions may mean martyrdom.

It is always a hard matter for a girl, however high her spirit may be, to set herself in direct opposition to her lawful governors—parental or otherwise. It is reading St. Paul's precepts upside down—giving them a contrary meaning; the 'Children, obey' seems to tingle in her ears ever after. Gerda had plenty of spirit, but she was gentle by nature, and had been brought up in a good old-fashioned way; she had an invincible dislike to hurt anyone's feelings, especially the feelings of those who were set in authority over her. She would inveigh against them in her honest, downright fashion—she might even air her weapons of sarcasm and girlish obstinacy; but when the moment of decision came, the disappointment she must inflict would give her intense pain.

'I am too thin-skinned,' she said to herself with a sigh; 'one's nature ought to be more tough when one has an unpleasant duty to perform. I know it will make me miserable to disappoint Grand, but I ought not to mind that. The question is, Is it my duty to marry Gerard?' But even as she asked herself the question, she dismissed it with a sudden shrug of impatience. 'I will marry Nobody—Nobody will be the best,' she said to herself, as she prepared to leave her room.

She lingered a moment on the staircase as Doris's voice reached her ear—staccato with horrified amazement:

'Oh, Gerard, how horrible!'

Gerda looked over the balustrade from the same point of view that Dr. Lyall had chosen the previous night; the hall was neutral territory, and was not considered a place for secrets. Gerda had no scruples of conscience as she leant against the carved oak balustrade, and calmly contemplated the couple who were so cosily ensconced on the seat in the oriel window. They were far too much occupied to notice the interloper. Gerard was polishing a pair of skates, and telling his story at the same time, and Doris's curly head was very near him; she had a small black kitten in her arms—which was known in the family by the name of Methuselah—and her cheek rested against the sooty coat of the little animal as she watched the process of skate-polishing.

'Of course it was rather awkward,' went on Gerard, as he paused to admire the results of his labour. Gerard's hands were never idle; the lounging, feckless ways of most young men were abhorrent to him; his spare indoor hours were always well employed.

His den, as he called it—a large cheerful room opening out of the hall—held numerous tokens of his industry—a lathe, a photographic apparatus, and a half-finished fishing-net, while various specimens of carving, and materials for making flies, bore witness to the fact that Gerard liked to vary his employments.

Doris had always taken an intelligent

interest in these pursuits; nothing pleased her better than an invitation to the den to help Gerard tie flies, or to watch him at his lathe; he was always so engrossed by his work, and he whistled over it in such a light-hearted fashion, she often wondered why Gerda did not share her interest. When Gerda entered the den, it was generally with an air of protest, and a shrug over its untidiness; she hinted at times that Gerard might find better employment than cleaning his gun or carving ugly little chessmen.

'You are always too busy to open a book, Gerard,' she would say sometimes. 'Carving is all very well, but you never find time to read ; you let your mind rust.'

Gerard always took these reproofs very lightly. He was no reader ; he was obliged to confess that the serious books that Gerda loved would have bored him excessively; the paper, or an exciting novel when he was tired or lazy, constituted Gerard's literature.

'Everyone to his own taste, my fair Saxon,' he would say good-humouredly ; 'one man's meat is another man's poison. Why cannot we agree to differ ? You are a sensible girl—just answer me that. I don't quarrel with you for your infatuation for Carlyle and Emerson, but you should not be down on a fellow because he prefers tying flies to all the essays that ever were written.'

'I am not quarrelling with you, Gerard,' Gerda would answer rather sadly, 'and I would not interfere with any of your favourite pursuits for the world; but it is the duty of every human being to improve his or her mind. How are you to hold your own among other men if you let yourself rust like this?'

But Gerda might as well have talked to the wind. Gerard never contradicted her; he even suffered her to put some favourite author on his table beside his pipes and tackle; but the weeks passed, and the book was never opened.

'Well, it was awkward, you know,' went on Gerard, feeling a certain pleasant zest in Doris's wide blue eyes and riveted attention; 'and I confess I felt pretty bad at that moment, and wished I had held my tongue. There was no one near us in the shanty, and he was such a big, hulking ruffian, with a fist that might have felled an ox; and the liquor he had taken had not improved his temper, you see. A bowie-knife is not a pleasant weapon, and he had a revolver besides, while Seymour and I had not even a stick between us.

'" I'll teach you, stranger, to insult an American citizen!" he begins, with a horrid grin—I can see the brute now—and out came the knife. Well, what does Seymour do?—you know what a dapper little fellow Seymour is, hardly up to my shoulder, but as cool as brass—he is a plucky chap is Seymour!

'" My dear sir," he said, stepping between us as quietly as possible, " don't take any notice of this poor fellow;" and here he actually tapped his forehead in a very significant way. " Brain-fever, you know, from over-work; could not be trusted anywhere alone; contradicts and argues with every man he sees; part of the disease; half my day's work to make apologies; wanted to argue with the German Emperor once, and the Portuguese Ambassador; sad case, very; only son of a widowed mother, and considered incurable." Well, the little idiot went on in this way until our Texas friend was persuaded to pocket his bowie-knife, and shake hands; and we had a big drink all round after that.'

'He actually believed that Mr. Seymour was your keeper?'

'My dear girl, he was half drunk, you see; and then I took Seymour's cue, and put on a vacant look. I always tell Seymour that his bit of cheek saved both of our lives. I am pretty strong, you know, but, still, a revolver soon puts an end to a fellow.'

At this point Gerda thought it time to interfere.

'Why do you tell Doris those sort of stories?' she observed reproachfully. 'You have made her look quite pale; she will dream of it to-night, and wake me up by calling out in her sleep.'

'Oh, you are there, are you, fair Saxon?' observed Gerard, quite unabashed at this rebuke.

If he had glanced round at Doris he would have discovered for himself that Gerda was right. Doris was biting her pretty lips to keep back the tears; she was a tender-hearted little soul, and was easily moved. Gerard had been in danger—in real, actual danger. This thought prevented her from perceiving the humour of the story.

'I wish I had known this when Mr. Seymour was here last week,' she remarked, a little shakily. 'I am sorry now that I said I did not care for him much; I would have been ever so much nicer to him.'

'Then you would have made him more conceited than he is already,' retorted Gerda, who had joined them and seated herself by Doris. 'I wonder why little men have always such a good opinion of themselves. With all your faults, Gerard, you are not a bit conceited. Now, Mr. Seymour talks as though his opinion was worth more than most people's.'

'He is a cheeky little beggar,' observed Gerard, under his breath; 'but he is a good sort, you know.'

'I dare say you know best,' returned Gerda, rather indifferent, 'as he is your friend, or chum. I think you prefer the latter word; it is very expressive, very: it means so much and so little. For my own part, I did not find him interesting; his conversation was limited. We did not have many points of sympathy, I fancy.'

'Why do you always abuse Gerard's friends?' retorted Doris, quite forgetting that she had also professed indifference to Mr. Seymour. 'They are very nice, only you are so fond of finding fault with people; you want a little world of your own—doesn't she, Gerard?'

'In that case, I am afraid Seymour and I, and the rest of the other fellows, would be cast into limbo,' observed Gerard, with a rueful glance at his cousin's calm face. 'You see, we are not up to the mark in Gerda's eyes. Well, even a worm will turn, and I mean to have my say. Seymour might be better for a few more inches, and he is not what you girls would call a good-looking fellow; but he is an honest, plucky little chap, and he did me a good turn that day, and I don't mind saying that I am grateful to him.'

'You are quite right to stick to him,' returned Gerda magnanimously, and Doris echoed indignantly, 'Of course he is;' and then the luncheon-bell sounded, and Doris jumped up at once, but the others did not follow her.

Gerard was putting the final polish to his

skates. Gerda hesitated for a moment, and then rose from her seat, and touched him lightly on his shoulder. Her quick woman's instinct had detected the hurt tone of his voice. With all his easy good-nature, Gerard was not invulnerable; he looked up a little gravely as she touched him.

'I did not mean to be hard on your friend, Gerard; I am afraid you are just a little bit hurt with me because I said Mr. Seymour was conceited.'

'Oh, it was not that,' he returned, for this little apology mollified him at once. 'Seymour lays himself open to that sort of remark, and he certainly has a tolerably good opinion of himself. I only wish sometimes that you cared more for the people and things I care about; it comes into my head sometimes, when you talk about other fellows, that you feel a cut above us all, and though it is true, it rather depresses one to hear it.'

'What nonsense!' returned Gerda, with one of her rare sunny smiles. 'I think you ever so much better than I. What can have put this in your head, you foolish fellow? Please ask Mr. Seymour down again, and you shall see how prettily Doris and I will behave to him. Only you do look such a giant beside him. Come, we must not keep Grand and mother waiting. Put down those skates; they really look as bright as silver—oh, they are mine! Thank you so much, Gerard; but I am afraid I shall not want to skate again for a long time.'

'Oh yes, you will! You are not going to funk skating just because of that tumble yesterday. I will take you on next time. I am not going to let another man get the pull of me. I shall not trust you out of my sight;' and with these words Gerard passed his arm through hers, and led her into the dining-room, where the rest of the family were awaiting them.

CHAPTER VII.

A TROUBLESOME PATIENT.

'We are always the martyrs of our own faults.'
CARMEN SYLVA.

GERDA received an unusual amount of attention during luncheon, which she appropriated with outward meekness and inward compunction; the consciousness of secret revolt made her unwilling to accept overmuch kindness. She was accustomed to a great deal of petting from her mother. Mrs. Meredith was prodigal of caresses and soft speeches to the objects of her affection. She was a woman who demanded perpetual assurance and sympathy, and it never entered her head that other and more reticent natures might be willing to dispense with much outward observance. Doris never wounded her with a repulse, but at times she was heard to lament somewhat mournfully over Gerda's indifference.

'It's only her manner,' Doris would say, for she always fired up in her sister's defence. 'People misunderstand Gerda because she is so very quiet, and says so little; but she is really affectionate.'

If Mrs. Meredith were prone to overmuch softness and indulgence, Sir Godfrey erred in the opposite direction. He had been brought up in the good old school, as he called it, and held the opinion that an occasional snubbing was wholesome for young people; so he seldom praised. In reality, he was both fond and proud of his young granddaughters, and thought no girls were to be compared to them; but he rarely permitted himself to indulge in any expression of endearment. They were good girls—he had not a word to say against them; but even young women were the better for a strong hand over them, and he thanked Heaven that he had too much good sense to spoil them, as that foolish mother of theirs was bent on doing.

Both the girls loved their grandfather, in spite of his strictness and arbitrary ways. They were clear-sighted enough to see through the irritating film of perpetual fault-finding, and to read the old man's heart aright.

'Grand ought to have been a Pharisee, with his everlasting mint and cumin of continual small observances,' Gerda once remarked scornfully. 'He is a stickler for the minor morals. Don't open your eyes, Gerard! Of course you do not know what I mean. Did you not once tell me you hated parables out of the Bible—I mean not in it?—oh, don't laugh! Everyone makes a mistake sometimes. You know you are not quick at grasping an idea.'

'Because I like plain English, that is no reason for calling me an idiot,' retorted Gerard, with a pretended growl—but all the same he suppressed a sigh. Gerda was too clever for him, he thought. He was not more stupid than other fellows; he knew a lot more on certain subjects than she did—how to make the most killing sort of flies, for example, or to play cricket or golf—but in talking she had the pull of him. Some of her speeches went over his head. And then he comforted himself with the assurance that when he was a married man he need stand no nonsense from his wife. 'I shall have to tell her to shut up sometimes, when she bores me too much with her books; but I dare say she will find other things to interest her then;' and Gerard's cheek glowed a little, for he was beginning to regard Sir Godfrey's scheme with a great deal of pleasure; in spite of her nonsense, he had not seen a girl who could hold a candle to her.

But in spite of Sir Godfrey's strictness, there were times when he would relax, and make himself exceedingly pleasant to his womankind. On the present occasion he was in an unusually genial mood. Perhaps the sight of Gerard and his cousin coming into the room in that free-and-easy fashion pleased him, and put him in a good humour.

'I do not see why we should not do it,' he observed mysteriously, as Gerda kissed him. 'The girls ought to have a treat sometimes;' and then Doris clapped her hands, and she and her mother exchanged glances. 'I'll think over it, and let you know later on,' he continued, still more oracularly; for it was a principle with Sir Godfrey never to decide on any domestic arrangement without due reflection; it somehow added to his importance to take time for deliberation, and to keep people in suspense, waiting for his decision.

Gerda lifted her eyebrows slightly as she took her place. She knew what had been the subject of their conversation. All the houses round were full of guests; it was rather a gay time at Chesterton, and an evening or two before Gerard had had the audacity to propose a dance at the Hall. 'Just a small affair, Uncle Godfrey,' he remarked coolly—'small and early, you know —a sort of Cinderella affair. It would be no trouble at all—the girls and I would manage everything; so don't look so alarmed, Cousin Honoria. Why, we could not muster more than thirty people in these benighted parts; but I would have Seymour and Gilbertson and two or three other fellows down, and put them up somehow.'

'Oh, Gerard, what a delightful idea!' exclaimed both Gerda and Doris at once.

But Sir Godfrey had received the proposition rather coldly.

'I am not quite sure that I like the notion,' he had replied slowly. 'You are wrong, Gerard. It will involve your cousin Honoria in a great deal of trouble—a great deal of trouble—but you young folk never think of that. I can't let the children run away with the idea that it is a settled thing'—Sir Godfrey generally spoke of his grand-daughters as the 'children'; 'I will think over it and let you know, Gerard.'

And that night they had ventured to say no more. But it was evident to Gerda that the subject had been resumed, and Gerard was of the same opinion, for he gave Doris a knowing look as he unfolded his napkin. But, to the aggravation of the three young people, Sir Godfrey's thoughts were diverted at this moment by the excellence of some favourite dish that had just been placed before him, and the next moment his attention was attracted by Gerda's paleness.

'Well, my princess,' he said—for this was his name for her when he was in a special good humour—'I am afraid you are none the better for your ice-bath yesterday.—She looks palish, Honoria; give her a glass of wine, Gerard.—Yes, you must drink it, my dear, it will do you good. By the way, Lyall was here just now, and left his respects for you.'

'Dr. Lyall!' Gerda changed colour a little as she bent over her plate.

'Yes, dear,' observed Mrs. Meredith, for Sir Godfrey's attention was diverted again for a moment. 'I found him in the library with your grandfather when I came down from your room. He came to inquire after you, and to bring a message from Mrs. Hake. He seemed glad to hear that you were resting. "That is very sensible of her," he said at once, and he hoped you would not venture out to-day, as the wind was very cold. I must say I think it was very polite of him to call, but he said he could do no less after our hospitality yesterday.'

'It was very kind,' murmured Gerda.

'He seems a very pleasant, gentlemanly man. Your grandfather thinks we ought to ask him to dinner.'

But here Sir Godfrey interfered in his pompous way:

'I said I would think about it, Honoria; but that is no reason for you to speak of it as a settled thing; and if we carry out Gerard's absurd plan, another dinner will be out of the question—but there, I have not made up my mind. Gerda, I insist on your finishing that wine; it will put some colour into your cheeks.'

'Dr. Lyall stayed such a long time,' went on Mrs. Meredith hurriedly, with a nervous conviction that she had made a slip. 'You had quite a discussion—had you not, father?'

'Well, well, perhaps we had; and I think I taught him a thing or two. He is certainly a well-bred man, and has plenty of brains. I am afraid it is uphill work with him in his profession—at least, he said as much: did he not, Honoria? He is only a junior partner, and of course he has to make his connection. I wonder now why he was so confidential about himself, for he seems a reserved sort of man—eh, Gerard?'

'Decidedly so, I should say.'

'Oh, it was your fault, father,' interposed Mrs. Meredith eagerly. 'Don't you recollect saying that a doctor ought to be a married man?—and then Dr. Lyall laughed, and said that it would never do for him to think of a wife yet, as he was not rich enough to afford such a luxury.'

'Ah, that was it, was it? I am sure I have forgotten I said any such thing. But of course I was right. Reynolds never had half the practice he has now until he married; and I recollect now that I cited him as an example.'

'Dr. Lyall took your remark in very good part. Somehow I fancy he is not a marrying man—I do not suppose he is more than three-and-thirty—but there is rather the cut of the old bachelor about him.'

'Pooh! nonsense! What rubbish you women will talk!' returned Sir Godfrey peevishly, for he had finished his luncheon and was getting sleepy. 'I should not mind laying an even bet with anyone that Dr. Lyall will be a married man before two years are out.—There, ring the bell, Gerard; I want Stephens to see to the library fire—it is sure to be half out.' And at this decided hint the family dispersed.

Mrs. Meredith bustled off to the library, to see with her own eyes that the fire was in good condition, and Sir Godfrey's easy-chair put in its right position for the enjoyment of his afternoon nap; but the young people lingered for a few moments round the hall fire.

'Do you think Grand will give in about

the dance?' asked Doris anxiously, looking into Gerard's face.

'Give in! Why, it is a dead certainty. You and Gerda may write your invitations if you like.'

'Why, we do not even know the day. We could not do it—could we, Gerda? There is ever so much to settle beforehand.'

'Then it will have to be settled before twenty-four hours are over, as we must have the dance before next Wednesday. Let me see: to-day is Friday—we will fix Tuesday. All right! get the notes written, and I will settle it with Uncle Godfrey this evening.'

'Oh, Gerard, will you really!' and Doris looked at him with admiring gratitude. When Gerard said he would settle a thing, the thing was as good as done.

'Yes, of course I will; and now just hurry up, there's a good child, or we shall lose the best part of the afternoon;' and, as Doris ran off obediently, for she was docile, and a word from Gerard was enough for her, he continued: 'What are you going to do with yourself, Gerda? Shall I wheel up the big couch for you to take a nap?—for you don't look very fit, you know.'

'No, thank you,' she returned languidly; 'I could not possibly sleep to order; perhaps I shall come out presently and criticise your skating.'

'You must do nothing of the kind,' he returned decidedly; 'but, of course, you are not serious.' And, as Gerda made no response to this, he gave her a nod and a smile, and went off in search of Doris and his skates.

Gerda hardly knew if she were serious or not, but she was in a strange, unsettled frame of mind. The big couch that Gerard had suggested offered her no allurements, and in spite of the bleak, wintry air outside, and the gray sunless atmosphere, she had a restless desire to be out—a morbid fancy to see the spot where she had suffered such deadly terror and peril overmastered her common-sense.

'If I look at it again it will not haunt me to-night,' she thought, with swift, illogical reasoning; and, as usual with Gerda, impulse carried the day. Her mother, Gerard, and Dr. Lyall would all think her extremely foolish, but from certain points of view rashness seems the wisest course; it was worth while undergoing some risk to secure an easy night.

Gerda did not at once carry out her intention. She waited until her mother had betaken herself to the morning-room to write letters; then she slipped upstairs and wrapped herself up warmly, and went round to the stable-yard in search of her usual walking companion — a large white fox-terrier, with a black patch over one eye, who was Gerda's special property. No one was disposed to dispute her rights. Waif was by no means a prepossessing animal, and there were plenty of pets at the Hall. Mrs. Meredith had a pug, and Doris a small gray Skye, while Gerard was the owner of a St. Bernard and two knowing little fox-terriers, both of perfect breed and beauty.

Waif was a mongrel; he had begun life on a very humble scale, and past troubles and semi-starvation had given him a gaunt, veteran look. Gerda had seen him once or twice slinking with dejected tail at the heels of his master, a drunken tinker with a heavy hand and an irritable temper, and had been struck by the pathetic look of misery on the dog's face; perhaps the black patch added to this impression, and the distinct form of the ribs under the rough white coat. The third time she saw him Waif had hurt his foot; he had cut himself with a piece of broken glass, and sat under a hedge whining dismally, while his master cursed him from afar as he mended a kettle. Gerda's soft heart was full of pity for the poor animal, and in her impulsive way she stepped up to the tinker and offered him half a crown for the dog.

'You shall have him for five shillings,' was the surly response; and Gerda took out her purse and paid him on the spot.

'Will he follow me, do you think?' she asked timidly.

'I think he will,' was Joe Atkinson's answer, as, with a favourite oath, he took up a stone, at the sight of which Waif put his tail between his legs, and ran away as fast as his wounded foot allowed him.

Gerda started off in pursuit; the man's fiendish cruelty made her feel sick.

'Here, poor fellow!' she exclaimed, holding out her hand, as she reached him, panting slightly. 'No one shall hurt you. Come home with me; you are my dog now.'

It may be doubted whether Waif understood this speech, but there was one thing plain to his canine sagacity—that this young lady meant to deal kindly by him. He stood regarding her mournfully for a moment; such blandishments were new to his experience. Then his tail wagged feebly, and he suffered her to approach him and pat his rough coat; finally, he responded to her call and limped after her. Once or twice he looked back, as his conscience accused him of infidelity to his hard master; but each time the tinker's hand was uplifted, and when a flint stone skimmed along the path in unpleasant proximity to his hind-legs, Waif made up his mind that he had received his discharge, and was free to enter into another service.

Gerda conveyed him to the stable-yard, and, summoning the groom to her assistance, bathed the wounded foot, and provided the first sufficient meal that Waif had ever enjoyed since his mother left him to the mercies of a cruel world.

'He is a young dog, and when I have brushed him up a bit he will look a sight better,' remarked Felton; 'but he isn't the sort of a dog for a lady. Perhaps one of us could find him a home.'

Waif was in the delicious enjoyment of a bone at that moment, which he was gnawing as only a hungry dog could gnaw; but, as Felton made this sensible speech, he dropped the bone, and looked up in Gerda's face with mute reproach.

'No, no; I mean to keep him,' she replied hurriedly, in response to this mute appeal; and then, as Waif wagged his tail and returned to his bone, she went on: 'He is not handsome, of course, but he looks clever. I am sure, Felton, he understands what we say; please take care of him, and do not let the other dogs worry him, and I will come and see him again.'

From that day Waif was her devoted slave. Gerda never repented her bargain with the tinker, and she bore with calm philosophy the unfavourable criticisms on her favourite. 'Waif cares nothing about his looks, neither do I,' she would say. 'He is as good as gold, and he seems to understand everything I say to him.' Gerda would willingly have had him as an inmate of the Hall, and she pleaded piteously with her grandfather and Gerard to be allowed to bring him in, but neither of them would listen to her.

'Two dogs are enough in a house,' the latter assured her. 'Waif is much better where he is; Felton will look after him, and you can take him for walks.'

'If I ever have a house of my own, I will take care that Waif has a warm corner in it,' Gerda was provoked to answer, and she wondered why Gerard laughed and shrugged his shoulders.

'That depends on the master,' he said to himself as he went off.

Waif had been in his present comfortable quarters for six months now, and though he was still somewhat gaunt, his condition had wonderfully improved, and his coat was almost as glossy as were those of the two terriers, Castor and Pollux. When he saw his mistress enter the yard he uttered a delighted bark and rushed to meet her, and Gerda found it difficult to prevent him from nearly upsetting her with his rough gambols.

And so it was that, somewhat later in the afternoon, Dr. Lyall, who had detached himself from the rest of the skaters to practise the outside edge in comfort, became aware of a tall gray figure standing at the far end of the lake, with a white dog sitting on his haunches beside her. He had keen eyes, and what he saw made him hastily retire and take off his skates, and ten minutes later a quiet and slightly sarcastic voice said in her ear:

'Do you always take such good care of yourself, Miss Meredith?'

Gerda started, and turned round. Her eyes had a dazed, uncertain look in them. Their expression made Dr. Lyall's next speech more than usually brusque.

'Do you think it prudent to stand in this north-east wind for a quarter of an hour at a time?' he continued. 'I am afraid you have small regard for your health. Why, you look half frozen. Please come back with me at once to the Hall. You are making yourself quite ill.'

Dr. Lyall's tone of displeased remonstrance roused Gerda effectually, and she quietly accompanied him. For the first two or three minutes neither of them spoke.

Dr. Lyall, who was a plain, practical man, felt himself annoyed by the girl's perversity. He had recommended warmth and rest, and instead of taking his advice she was standing, looking as pale as death, by the lake-side, and when he had spoken to her she had seemed half dazed. He felt inclined to take no further trouble about her. Evidently she was one of those morbid, hysterical girls whose selfwill is stronger than their common-sense. Of course, he had no right to be angry; but as a medical man——

But here his reflections were interrupted by a soft, unsteady laugh.

'Dr. Lyall, you have only known me for four-and-twenty hours, and this is the second time you have found me doing a foolish thing.'

'I fear that I must endorse that statement, Miss Meredith,' he replied shortly. 'I am a plain man, and I think it best to tell the truth. You are certainly acting very unwisely; you might take a serious chill.'

'I don't think I shall; but I am very cold.' And, indeed, her teeth were chattering as she spoke. 'Of course I deserve what I get, but I should hate to be ill, all the same. Doris and I are never ill. Dr. Lyall,' laughing timidly up into his grave face, 'please don't think me more foolish than you can help. I want to tell you something. I came out just to look at the place where I went in yesterday. I thought if I saw it again it would not haunt me. It was in my dreams last night, and I thought——' Here she paused with a wistful air, as though she wanted him to understand her.

'Was it necessary to brave the bleak wind for a morbid idea?' he asked. But his tone had grown more gentle. This childlike confession disarmed him.

'It was necessary for my peace of mind,' she returned quietly. 'I must always face a thing at once. It is difficult for a man to understand. We women are such cowards—our imaginations are too much for us. When I was a child I was always like that; however frightened I was, I could not run away from my bogie. I remember once waking up and seeing a dark shape in my room. It looked like an old man in a long cloak. I was sick with terror. In my place any other child would have hidden her head under the bedclothes; but I sprang out of bed at once and made for the thing. Of course it was only an effect of moonlight on the curtain, so I was rewarded for my effort, and could go to sleep happily.'

'You must have been an extremely plucky little girl.'

'Not at all,' very decidedly. 'It was sheer cowardice. I wanted to know the worst; but I was horribly frightened all the time.'

'I maintain the contrary, Miss Meredith. Do you know a brave soldier will own to fear in his first battle? I remember a man telling me—and he was one of the pluckiest fellows I ever knew—that as he and his detachment were drawn up waiting for the enemy's charge, his only dominant feeling was fear. "I funked the whole thing," was his expression; "it was one of the most unpleasant moments of my life." But when the enemy was on them, and they had their orders to fire, he had no fear. I am afraid I shall shock you when I tell you that my friend owned that he experienced a sort of mad joy and excitement. "It was splendid while it lasted, but it was over in no time. Our fellows drove the rascals back in five minutes." That is how he summed it up. You see, man is a fighting animal, Miss Meredith.'

'It seems so,' was her quiet reply. And then, to her relief, they reached the Hall, and as Dr. Lyall placed a chair for her beside the blazing fire, she sank into it with a sigh of relief.

'I did not know how cold I was,' she murmured, as she stretched out her hands to the pleasant warmth.

Rogers was arranging the tea-table as they entered, for a large party from the lake was expected. Dr. Lyall coolly helped himself to a cup of tea, and brought it to Gerda.

'You had better drink that,' he said rather authoritatively, for there was a blue tint round the girl's lips that made him uneasy. She took it with a smile, and the next moment they could hear voices and footsteps approaching up the avenue.

CHAPTER VIII.

WON BY THE MAJORITY.

'What is the use of a fine collar if it strangles you?'
Proverb of Montenegro.

A MINUTE later there was a rush of cold air, the clatter of high-heeled boots on the polished oak floor, and the old hall was filled with a bevy of bright young faces, while their chaperons, Captain and Mrs. Hake, followed more leisurely, with a tall, slim young man in clerical dress, with a round, boyish face and closely-cropped fair head, who was no other than the new curate—Rev. Bertram Allingham. In a moment Gerda was surrounded, and there was a chorus of mingled exclamations, congratulations, and ejaculations of sympathy and horror, which was proof enough to Dr. Lyall that Miss Meredith was a favourite with her young companions.

'I am so sorry, Gerda dear. Mamma and I have hardly slept a wink thinking of the danger you escaped.'

'Why, how did you hear of it, Robina?'

'Oh, Andrews, our odd man, picked it up from your groom, and he told Marvel. You can imagine our feelings! I wanted papa to go off then and there to the Hall; but he had his slippers on, and was too lazy. He said you must be all right, or we should have heard; but I could not sleep for ever so long;' and here Robina, a pretty little brunette, stole a look at Dr. Lyall from under her dark lashes.

'Dear Gerda, I am so thankful!' whispered a tall girl who had not hitherto spoken. This was Frances Hilton, the Vicar's daughter, and report said that she and the boyish-faced young curate were on the eve of an engagement. She was a quiet, gentle-looking girl, and as she spoke her eyes were full of tears.

'My congratulations were all given last night,' exclaimed Mrs. Hake in her loud, cheerful voice, as she pressed through the group of girls. 'Somebody told me that you had been seen flitting round the lake like a gray ghost, and as you have your hat on, I am afraid it is true. You look shockingly, Gerda—but I expect it is all your fault. I would not be in your mother's shoes for anything; I am sure you girls lead her a life.— Is that cup of tea for me, Mr. Allingham? No—no sugar, thank you. I am getting too stout, my husband says, and sugar is so fattening.—Now, Doris, what is this that a little bird has just told me about a Cinderella dance at the Hall? Well, if you must know, Mr. Hamlyn gave me a hint of it.'

'It was in strict confidence, Mrs. Hake,' observed Gerard, who had overheard this, and was passing with a plate of cake. 'Don't let Cousin Honoria hear you.'

'She has heard us already—she is shaking her head at us. Look, girls, I have a grand idea! Let us all go and beard Sir Godfrey in his library. He will not be able to resist us. I will make a speech, and you shall all back me up. Come, Edith, Constance, Doris, Robina—Gerda, you have an invalid's privilege, but we will not dispense with Frances—Mr. Allingham, if you can spare Miss Hilton!'—and Frances rose at once with a blush. 'Pamela, why are you keeping your seat?'

But that vivacious young lady shook her head.

'I am not coming, Gertrude, thank you. I want the dance as badly as any of you, but I know my place as a stranger. Alick agrees with me—don't you, Alick? The deputation will be complete without me.'

Dr. Lyall nodded. The little scene amused him, and he was glad to see that Gerda had thrown off her lassitude, and looked pleased and interested. As Mrs. Hake swept the chattering, laughing girls before her out of the room, he left his place and joined the three gentlemen at the tea-table. To his surprise, they were quietly and seriously discussing the dance.

'I shall have to look on, you know; you must not count on me,' observed Mr. Allingham, in a regretful tone. 'The Vicar does not approve of his curates dancing.'

'Nonsense, my dear fellow! A small affair like this: half a dozen couples—well, a dozen, then,' as the curate looked mildly surprised at this reckoning. 'Besides, we will not split on you.'

And then Captain Hake took up the argument.

'Dancing is the finest exercise in the world, after tennis and that sort of thing. All the medical faculty recommend it—eh, Lyall?'—with a playful poke in the ribs. 'You should not be so strait-laced, Allingham. We look for liberality and breadth of opinion from a Merton man. It would not be pleasant to your feelings to see Miss Augusta or Miss Frances sitting in the corner for want of a partner. Come, now, there's an appeal to your chivalry!' and Bertram Allingham confessed that, under those circumstances, he might be inclined to hesitate.

Meanwhile, Pamela had drawn her chair to the edge of the big bearskin rug, and had plunged into a conversation in her usual abrupt fashion. She was looking very pretty, Gerda thought; the dark ruby dress and hat exactly suited her dark complexion, and the exercise had brightened her eyes and heightened her colour.

'I saw you down by the lake an hour ago, Miss Meredith, and I was not a bit surprised when Alick took off his skates to go to you. He would disapprove of the whole thing—sentiment and all. He ordered you home at once, did he not? That was Alick all over.'

'He certainly told me that it was unwise to stand still so long—the wind was so dreadfully cold. I am afraid he thought me very silly.'

'Of course he did. Alick thinks most women are born without common-sense; he has not a grain of sympathy for what he calls false sentiment. But you and I think differently. In your place I should have done just the same; it is not every day that one lives through such a moment as that. It must be delicious to go through it all again—on the same spot, too.'

Gerda stared at her. Was the girl serious, or was she secretly making fun of her? She did not quite like Pamela's tone—it was rather too sarcastic.

'You quite misunderstand my motives,' she began rather stiffly.

But Pamela checked her with a light laugh:

'My dear Miss Meredith, I should never misunderstand you. I grasped the whole situation last night. We are alike in one thing, we are both intense; you are always so terribly in earnest, are you not?'

'Not more than other people.'

'Oh dear yes! How can you make such a mistake! Now, I am only earnest by fits and starts, but we are both intense, for all that. I could prove it to you in ten minutes, but I won't, for fear of boring you. Alick is not a bit intense; he is matter-of-fact and practical—that is why we quarrel sometimes.'

'I hope you are not serious!'

'I am perfectly so, I assure you. Alick is terribly damping sometimes; I get hobbies, and then he tries to crush me with some common-sense remark, as he calls it; then I flare up, and then, sometimes, I won't speak to him for the rest of the day.'

'I am inclined to pity Dr. Lyall.'

'I expected you to say that. Hester pities him, too; she always takes his part.'

'May I ask who Hester may be?'

'Well, as you ask so very prettily, I don't mind telling you. Hester is my sister; she is older than I. A good many years ago she made an unfortunate marriage—at least, Alick says so—but I own I am very fond of my brother-in-law; he is a cousin of Mr. Vincent's

—my *fiancé*, I mean,' as Gerda looked at her in a questioning manner. 'I suppose Gertrude told you I am engaged; she tells everybody. I never knew a woman who advocates matrimony so strongly; but I am not quite sure that I agree with her.'

'I thought you just told me you were engaged,' returned Gerda, rather bewildered by this last remark.

'So I am, and so I have been for the last three years; but I am just as likely to remain Pamela Lyall to the end of the chapter. I dare say you think my speech a little enigmatical; but, in this vexatious world, money is a great power—and, unfortunately, neither the Vincents nor the Lyalls have much of it. Unhappily, there is this difference between the cousins: Derrick would work hard if he could only get work to do, but he has not had a single brief yet; and Julius, my brother-in-law, hates work, and does as little as he possibly can.'

'Is your brother-in-law a lawyer, too?'

'No, he is an artist—and not a very good artist, either; at least, people will not buy his pictures. Alick says he does not take pains to find out what will please the public taste.

He just works in a groove; now and then he wakes up and paints a pot-boiler, as Hester calls it.'

'It sounds rather serious; it is to be hoped they have no children.'

'My dear Miss Meredith, you have a great deal to learn yet. Your question proves ignorance of the world; poor people always have children—have you never remarked that? They have two boys and a girl—the girl is a cripple, I am sorry to say.'

'You must be very sorry for your sister?'

'So I am—and I am sorry for Julius, too, he's such a good-looking fellow; and I do not believe that it is his fault as much as people say. There must be something defective in his moral nature. I am aware that I am playing the casuist, and that my remark touches on one of those nice and puzzling questions in what Alick terms the science of ethics; but I hold the opinion that certain human beings, my brother-in-law among them, are less accountable, or I should say more irresponsible, than other people. As long as Julius lives he will never be a full-grown man.'

'Is it not a pity that your sister married him?'

'My dear creature! Hester fulfilled her destiny, as you and I will fulfil ours. The Parcæ, commonly known as the Fates, do most of the spinning of the human web. If Hester had not married Julius, she would not have been Hester. That is how I put it.'

'You seem to be a fatalist.'

'I hardly know what I am. I am a poor little girl who wants to know everything—and knows nothing. Hush! I hear voices—what a procession!' and Pamela broke off her odd disjointed talk and began to laugh as Sir Godfrey entered the hall, with Mrs. Hake on his arm and Robina Stewart leading him by the hand, the other girls following him.

'Won by the majority, I see,' said Captain Hake, rubbing his hands.

'I gave in at once,' returned Sir Godfrey, with an old-fashioned bow to the company; 'when youth, beauty, and eloquence combine to make a fool of an old man,' and here there was a twinkle in his eye, 'there is no resistance possible.'

'Of course not. We "came, saw, and conquered"—did we not, Sir Godfrey?' cried

Robina roguishly, for she was an old favourite, and had often begged favours for Gerda and Doris when they were little girls, and she was used to making saucy little speeches. 'It is all right, Gerda. There is to be a Cinderella dance, and the day is to be fixed before we go. Sir Godfrey has behaved like an angel.'

'Sir Godfrey is going to open the ball with me, Lionel,' and Mrs. Hake looked at her husband. 'Now, Mr. Hamlyn, as it is an open secret, we will resolve ourselves into a committee of ways and means—we are all friends here. Pamela, my dear, you may go away—no one wants you. Mrs. Meredith, your father has bespoken my help; he wishes me to advise you on one or two points, especially——' Here Mrs. Hake lowered her voice as she seated herself beside Mrs. Meredith, and Gerda, in her distant corner, heard no more.

'Are you fond of dancing, Miss Meredith?' asked Dr. Lyall, coming up to her at this moment.

'Oh yes; all girls like dancing—and most men too: my cousin Gerard is devoted to it. I hope you like it too?'

'Well, no—not especially, I mean'—as

Gerda looked a little disappointed. 'I don't mind looking on—a dance is always a pretty sight—but I should be wrong if I called myself a dancing man.'

'Then I am afraid you will be bored.'

'Oh no!' and Dr. Lyall's smile was a pleasant one; 'I am seldom bored, and I dare say I shall do my duty like a man. Are we to dance in this fine old hall on Wednesday night?'

And as Gerda nodded, Gerard came up to them with a very bright face.

'It is all settled, Gerda. Uncle Godfrey is like wax in Mrs. Hake's hands. She has got leave to bring all her nieces—even the red-haired Miss Nancy, whom Uncle Godfrey abhors; and I am to fill all the spare rooms with my special chums. I'll write to Seymour and Gilbertson and Drury at once.'

'I am so glad, Gerard! Doris will be so pleased—and it will be her first dance, too.'

'So it will!'—with evident surprise. 'I never thought of that. In that case you won't mind my asking her for the first dance. I should like to pay her that little attention, she is such a dear little soul.

Mind you keep three valses for me—three!
—I will not let you off with less.'

Gerard's tone was a trifle dictatorial, and he enforced his speech with a look that made Gerda turn to Dr. Lyall hastily and say :

' I suppose you can waltz ?'

' Well, I can get round the room somehow ; but I do not suppose my partner is particularly happy. Ah, I see Mrs. Hake is about to take her leave, so I may as well say good-bye ; but I wish you would promise one thing before I go ;' and as Gerda looked up at him with a soft, questioning smile ; ' that you will take more care of yourself, and not go near the lake to-morrow ;' and as she assented to this he dropped her hand a little hurriedly.

' Good-bye,' exclaimed Pamela, with a friendly look. ' We were interrupted in our nice talk, and must finish it another time. Are you waiting for me, Alick ? Very well, I will come ;' and Pamela tripped after him into the darkness outside.

' I like that girl, after all,' she said, as she took her brother's arm—a sisterly attention with which he would willingly have dispensed, for he wanted a chat with his friend Hake, and the offer of a cigarette from that obliging person. 'I was not quite sure of her last night; I thought that she was just a little bit affected; but I have found out my mistake. She is absolutely genuine.'

'Are you not a little premature in your criticism? You have only talked to Miss Meredith for two consecutive half-hours, and there you are, as usual, heaping a new acquaintance with every possible and impossible virtue.'

'If you are going to be disagreeable and sarcastic, Alick, I shall leave off talking. Don't you know there are people whom you seem to know thoroughly in an hour, while there are other people with whom you do not get intimate during a whole lifetime? This afternoon I discovered that Miss Meredith and I were in touch—that we thought alike on many points.'

'I rather wonder at that,' returned her brother ironically, for he did not believe this statement in the least. As far as he could judge during their very limited acquaintance, he thought no two girls could be more dissimilar than Pamela and Gerda Meredith.

'But she is terribly delicate,' went on Pamela, disregarding the sneer in Alick's tone. 'I should not like anyone in whom I was interested to take a fancy to her. He would have a sickly wife.'

'Nonsense!' was the blunt reply. 'She only looks ill from the chill and fright. Many people are naturally without much colour. I expect Miss Meredith is as strong as most women.'

'Oh, do you think so?' returned Pamela, who never ventured to contradict her brother on matters of health. Well, I am very glad to hear it. Let me see, someone was telling me last night—who could it be?—not Gertrude; no, it was Miss Dalton: the younger one, Augusta—yes, Augusta Dalton told me that Sir Godfrey—what an old beau he is, Alick!—is bent on making up a match between his nephew and Miss Meredith.'

Dr. Lyall gave a slight imperceptible start.

'Did you slip, Alick? Perhaps you have got some ice under your heel. Dear, dear, how tired I am! and you walk so dreadfully fast! Do you want to overtake the others?'

'No; it is only this beastly wind;' for Dr. Lyall was not in the best of tempers.

'Oh, I do not mind it in the least! Well, I am sure, if Augusta Dalton be correct, Miss Meredith is a lucky girl. Mr. Hamlyn is his uncle's heir; and then he is such a handsome fellow, and so pleasant and good-natured! I am sure he spent more than half an hour trying to teach that stupid little Robina Stewart the outside edge. What a little flirt she is! She was trying to fascinate him all the time—and then he helped that plain Miss Robins. He did not get a bit of fun himself.'

Dr. Lyall did not answer. Perhaps the subject did not interest him. Pamela always chattered away, whether he listened to her or not. What a gossip she was, to be sure! and he hated gossip. But later on that evening he caught himself wondering if she had spoken the truth. The story was a probable one; propinquity and convenience had a great deal to do with many marriages.

'I suppose it is true,' he said to himself, when he found himself alone. 'Not that it matters to me whether it is so or not.' And then he pulled off his boots and fell into a reverie.

When the guests had departed, Gerda still

sat by the fire wrapped in her furs. She was in a dreamy, quiescent mood. A sense of warmth, rest, and well-being stole over her. This was the hour she loved, only Rogers had lighted the lamps and spoiled the twilight.

Sir Godfrey was in his high-backed chair, with his pince-nez comfortably fixed on his nose, and his paper in his hand; but he was not reading. Gerard had been teasing Doris, a favourite employment with him, and now he had persuaded her to practise the new valse step with him, and Mrs. Meredith was playing by ear in the dark drawing-room; but, though the pedal was down, only a few faint sounds reached them.

'Never mind, I'll whistle the accompaniment, and you will be sure to keep time,' observed Gerard, making light of this difficulty.

Gerda watched the slowly revolving figures; then she started as her grandfather touched her. He regarded her benignly as he spoke.

'Gerard and Doris seem excellent friends, do they not?'

'Oh yes,' she answered cordially; 'Gerard is always so good to her, and she is very fond of him. How well she dances! but, then,

Gerard is such a nice partner. Does it not seem strange, Grand, that this will be Doris's first dance, and she is eighteen?'

'Humph! I do not see anything strange,' in rather a ruffled tone, 'about that,' for this was touching on a secretly sore point. 'Doris is a mere child still, and I do not hold with putting young girls forward. I told Hake so when he spoke to me.'

'Did Captain Hake talk to you about Doris?'

'It was not Doris specially, but he had the impertinence to tell me once that he thought it a great pity that I did not give my grand-daughters the advantage of a London season. As though my private affairs were any business of his! But Hake is always putting in his oar about one thing or another. I believe that clever wife of his is at the bottom of all the mischief.'

'But, Grand,' opening her eyes a little widely, 'it would be such an expense, a London season.'

'I suppose I could afford it if I chose,' in a dignified voice; 'but I have no wish to see you and Doris changed into fashionable young women. Gerard and I talked it over once, and to my surprise he agreed with me. He owned it would be great fun, but that it would spoil you for a country life. He said some of the men were such asses, and that he thought on the whole it would be a mistake —that it would only make you both discontented.'

' I think it was ridiculous of Gerard to say that. Doris and I ought to be presented;' and Gerda drew up her long neck and looked at her grandfather a little defiantly. Now and then she would give herself these little airs with him, but for once he forbore to snub her.

' Oh, that is your opinion, is it, my princess?' —still in high good humour—' but I am afraid you must wait for that until you are married. Don't you think that it is high time you were engaged, Gerda?' in rather a meaning tone. ' Why, you are one-and-twenty—your mother was married long before that. You see, my dear'—in an affectionate tone—' I am not a rich man, and I am trying to improve the property for Gerard. Gerard will be far better off than I am. Nothing would please me better than to see you and Doris well married; but of course it is your turn first.

Don't you think it about time to make up your mind? In that case I should not be surprised if a house in town might not be forthcoming for at least one season, and then Doris could come out under your wing. Your mother and I often talk of that. There are the Hamlyn jewels, you know; any bride might be proud of them——'

But Gerda could bear no more. Sir Godfrey had often dropped hints in her presence. There had been a word here and a word there that had pierced her consciousness, but he had never spoken so plainly. What! she was to be bribed to marry Gerard! A house in town, Doris's advantage, the Hamlyn diamonds, were to be offered to her as baits! Oh, what would Gerard say? Would not his simple manly honesty revolt at such bribes? She rose hurriedly.

'Rogers is just going to sound the gong. I must go now, please, or I shall not be ready for dinner.'

Gerda did not wait for permission. She fled past the two dancers upstairs and into her own room.

'Grandfather is too bad, too bad!' she said to herself with girlish indignation. 'He is growing old—indeed, he is in his dotage. Am I to be bought with a house in town? It is absurd—monstrous—inconceivable! But Gerard is no party to such a scheme. He would hate all this talk as much as I do.'

And Gerda dressed herself disconsolately, and there was a cloud on her young brow; the old difficulties had beset her again, and robbed her of her peace.

CHAPTER IX.

ON THE CHILVERTON ROAD.

'When in conversing with anyone you see that he is keeping something back, it seems as though you were feeling for his hands across a wall.'—CARMEN SYLVA.

THE dance at the Hall was regarded as a public event in Chesterton, and when, the next day, the frost suddenly showed signs of breaking up, there were fewer lamentations than usual on the part of the young folk, for, as Doris remarked triumphantly, it would not be quite useless now to send invitations to Stanix Park and Blacklea, as a five-mile drive would not be utterly impossible.

'Gerard says that he should not be surprised if we get about sixteen couples,' she observed to Gerda the following evening; 'and if we count the married people, we shall muster over forty;' and Doris's cheeks were pink with excitement as she spoke.

Gerda laid down her book, and regarded her sister with a sort of pitying amusement. Was Doris only three years younger than herself? Could it be only three years since her own eyes had brightened, and her heart palpitated at the idea of her first dance? What a different affair that had been! Sixteen couples, indeed! Why, it had been a ball at Queen's Gate, and the room had been full of officers. She remembered how their spurs had torn the ladies' dresses; Bertie Longhurst, the heir of Stanix Park, had just come of age, and his aunt, Lady Paget, had celebrated the event by a ball. It was the only glimpse of London gaiety Gerda had ever had, and she recalled even now the brief intoxication, the dreamy bewilderment, as her first partner, a young lieutenant in the hussars, whirled her over the polished floor to the delicious strains of one of Strauss' valses.

'Well, Gerda,' and Doris stamped her foot in pretended impatience, 'why are you smiling in that disdainful way, instead of answering me? I believe your wits are wool-gathering again.'

'I was reading the "Thoughts of a Queen,"' returned Gerda calmly. She rather loved to tease Doris by affecting a stoicism she did not feel. Nothing provoked Doris more than seeing Gerda put on elder-sisterly airs. 'She was such a wise young queen, Dorrie,' she continued, 'as wise as the Queen of Sheba after she had heard the wisdom of Solomon. Just listen to this racy little bit:

'"Imagination is a gay companion, who frolics along the road and tells us tales. Reality is an old woman, who talks of nothing but herself, and, always fatigued, wants to be carried.'

'What stupid stuff!' returned Doris, rather crossly, for she was in no mood for philosophical reflections. 'Why should Reality be an old woman? As though young people could not be real too! As for Imagination, you are ever so much more imaginative than I—Gerard said so once. Don't you recollect his calling us Poetry and Prose, and you were affronted because he said afterwards that he hated poetry?'

Gerda laughed; the little episode had

escaped her memory, but she recalled it now. How red Gerard had got after uttering that unlucky speech, and how abject had been his apology, 'I did not mean it, you know, not really'!

'Prose is the best for everyday life,' she had returned quietly; 'you are quite right, Gerard. I do not mind you telling the truth in the least. Doris is far nicer than I am; she is not always walking about with her head in the clouds.' But to this injudicious speech Gerard made no reply.

'Never mind, Doris; I will not tease you any more. What were you saying about sixteen couples? I hope you are not counting either Dr. Lyall or Mr. Allingham, for they will not dance.'

'Indeed they will!' replied Doris excitedly. 'Gerard says he will insist on every man doing his duty. What are we to do about dresses, Gerda? I suppose I must wear my white silk; I have nothing else;' and then the two girls began gravely discussing the contents of their wardrobe.

This conversation had taken place on Saturday evening; all the invitations had been sent out, and Gerard had telegraphed to several choice spirits who were sojourning in various parts of the country. The band, too, a cornet and pianist from the neighbouring town, had been bespoken, and an extensive order to the confectioner had been written by Mrs. Meredith, who was already nearly worn out by the minute and fussy orders that Sir Godfrey was giving every hour of the day.

Sir Godfrey felt himself to be a public benefactor. During the next few days the Master of Chesterton Hall was very much to the fore; nothing must be done without his surveillance; he must give every order, superintend every arrangement — even the polishing of the oak floor, and the decoration and lighting of the old hall, could not be carried out without his constant supervision. When Mrs. Hake and Pamela called to offer their assistance, the afternoon before the dance, they found Sir Godfrey standing before the fireplace with his pince-nez in his hand, directing Rogers and a bevy of maids, while Mrs. Meredith stood at his elbow putting in a timid word now and then, and looking excessively tired.

'Take care how you move that oak

cabinet, Rogers; it is just the least bit rickety on one foot.—Thank you, Gerard,' as that young man went to Rogers' help. —'Hannah, what are you doing with that china?—My dear,' turning to his daughter, 'you know I never allow the maids to touch the Sèvres china; Hannah has an awkward knack of letting things slip through her fingers. Where are the girls? It is their business.—Hannah, I insist on your not touching the contents of that cabinet! My granddaughters will be here directly. — Emma, tell the young ladies that I wish them to come at once.—Ah, Mrs. Hake, you find us busy—extremely busy—my daughter and I are superintending things. Servants are like children; they cannot be trusted out of one's sight. Rogers has no head.—Sit down, ladies.—Honoria, my love, will you take Mrs. Hake to the drawing-room? There is some sort of fire there, I believe, and Gerard and I will finish here.'

'Do let us stop and help,' entreated Mrs. Hake, taking no notice of this hint to withdraw. 'How admirably you have managed the lighting, Mr. Hamlyn! Those sconces and the evergreens look so well.—Dear me,

Sir Godfrey, you might be in the habit of giving dances every fortnight, you seem to understand the whole thing so well!'

'I believe we were indebted to Gerard for most of the suggestions,' returned Sir Godfrey graciously. Mrs. Hake knew how to manage him exactly: a word of praise, a smile and a glance, and he became at once lamb-like. 'We are raw recruits down here, Mrs. Hake; we want drilling; and Gerard is good enough to perform that office.—An eighth of an inch more to the right, Gerard'—with a wave of his hand—'just so—thank you. Now for the piano!—Doris, where is your sister? I want you to move the china—this is your department, I believe; it was quite against rules for Hannah to touch it—you and Gerda.'

'Gerda has gone out for a walk, Grand,' returned Doris, in rather a frightened tone. 'She was tired of all the bustle, and said it made her head ache. I persuaded her to go. I can do the china very well alone.'

'Nonsense! when we are here to help you,' returned Mrs. Hake vigorously, for a cloud had gathered on Sir Godfrey's brow.

'It is very odd that Gerda has a headache

whenever she is required to make herself useful,' he began; but Gerard, as usual, undertook the defence of the absent.

'Gerda has not seemed the thing since that confounded ice accident,' he observed, strolling across the hall with his hands in his pockets. 'We shall have you knocked up, too, Uncle Godfrey, if you stand about any longer. Go into the drawing-room and get some tea. — Mrs. Hake, please take him away—he never refuses a lady;' and Sir Godfrey at last allowed himself to be persuaded.—'We shall get on twice as fast without him,' Gerard observed confidentially to Pamela. 'The dear old boy fusses himself far too much.—Hannah, you need not go away; you can help Miss Doris. I am sure you will take care not to break things— and we really want hands.'

'Will mine do?' asked Pamela, in much humility, spreading out a pair of pretty little hands as she spoke. 'Will Mr. Hamlyn deign to accept my poor services?' and she dropped him a little curtsey.

'All right; Doris will find you something to do, Miss Lyall,' he returned good-humouredly, and he went off in search of

Rogers. He was not quite sure he admired Miss Lyall; she was very bright and piquante, but just a little too sharp for his taste; and then he wondered for the third time why Gerda should be prowling about the cold wet roads in the twilight. If he were not so busy he would go after her; he hated girls wandering about after dark.

He need not have concerned himself about her safety, for at that moment she was walking through the village with Dr. Lyall. He had come out of the gate as she was passing Braeside, and Waif had foolishly barked at him, thereby attracting his attention.

Gerda had seen Dr. Lyall each day; whether by accident or design, they had met continually. On Sunday he and Captain Hake had walked home with them from church, and had been persuaded by Sir Godfrey to stay to luncheon. They had spent the remainder of the afternoon dawdling over the fire in pleasant desultory conversation; Dr. Lyall had been drawn into a discussion on books, and Gerda found that he knew most of her favourite authors.

'I am rather an omnivorous reader,' he confessed. 'I read everything that comes to hand; but I suppose I have my tastes, like other people;' and after a little judicious pressing on Gerda's part, he had named two or three books that had long been her favourites.

'Dr. Lyall is very intelligent,' she had remarked to her sister after the two gentlemen had taken their leave. 'It is a little difficult to get at his opinions, as he is naturally reserved, but I can see that he thinks deeply on some subjects.'

'I am glad you were pleased,' replied Doris dryly; 'but I cannot say that I found the conversation interesting. I liked Gerard's and Captain Hake's much better. I am never out of my depth with them.'

Gerda was not sorry when she saw Dr. Lyall's brisk, alert figure come out of Braeside; she looked upon him now as quite an old acquaintance. Dr. Lyall on his part looked excessively pleased.

'You have chosen a miserable afternoon for a walk,' he said, with an approving glance, notwithstanding, at her neat, trim appearance and thick boots. 'Do you always take a constitutional in all weathers?'

'I believe so; it is no use staying indoors,

unless it rains very heavily. But I confess it is not a pleasant afternoon.'

'You are putting it mildly,' he returned, as he suited his pace to hers; 'most people would use a stronger epithet, and I should not blame them '—looking before him at the half-melted slush of the road, and the dank, wet vegetation. It was a cold thaw, and the damp chill seemed to creep to his bones. 'We must walk fast if we are to keep warm,' he finished.

'Do not let me take you out of your way,' observed Gerda, a little nervously. 'I am quite used to walking alone. There was such a noise and bustle in the house that I was glad to escape; besides, my head ached.'

'I am afraid you sat up reading too late last night. Ah, I see you are startled at my singular penetration; but I am right for once, am I not? No, you are not taking me out of my way, for the sole reason that I have no way. I had just come out for a prowl. If you do not object to my companionship, I should like to accompany you. I want to point out to you seriously the error of your ways. Do you know that you are very sensitive and excitable, and that you need anodynes, not stimulants. Now, though I am no magician, I will wager anything you like that you had no beauty sleep last night.'

'I was certainly not in bed until one o'clock,' replied Gerda, in rather a guilty tone; 'but I assure you that I was not reading.'

'You were thinking, then?'

Gerda nodded.

Dr. Lyall threw up his head in rather an argumentative manner. Miss Meredith might be interesting and attractive, and in his opinion she was both; but she was not exempt from the weaknesses of her sex.

'I suppose you were thinking about the dance?'—and there was latent disdain in his tone. 'That is why I say you are excitable. A well-balanced mind——' But she interrupted him indignantly.

'The dance! Do you think I am a child? What an opinion you must have of me! As though the prospect of a pleasant evening would deprive me of sleep! You are wrong for once, Dr. Lyall,' walking on faster than ever, and her words tripping each other up, while he listened with an amused smile. 'I was thinking of far different things, of a much graver subject—I was wondering why so little light came to one when one was perplexed and could see no way out of the maze. After all, it is better to be a man. Men are so free; they can do what they like; no one ventures to control their actions; but when one is only a girl, people think they have a right to interfere — they give her advice, they thwart, and guide, and push her in every direction except where she wishes to go. I know people call this the emancipated age; but I do not seem to see it myself.'

'Does this deluge of strong indignation, that has almost swamped me, mean personal and grievous experience, or are you merely standing up in generous championship for the rights of your sex?'

'I see you are laughing at me, Dr. Lyall,' calming down under that cool, satirical tone; 'but I assure you that it is no matter for amusement. I am beginning to think women have a great deal to bear.'

'I will agree with you for once—suppose I give you that point; but we must not go too fast. You want to prove to me that the young women of the present age are still shackled, that their friends and relatives are often dictatorial and interfering. Perhaps in individual cases this may be so; but surely the girl is a free agent. There is no need for her to follow advice implicitly. After all, I do not think we need pity them. English girls are remarkably robust.'

'It is impossible for you to understand,' returned Gerda, with a sort of despair in her voice, which gave Dr. Lyall a painful sensation. 'You are not a woman; you do not comprehend the situation in the least.'

'Perhaps if you were a little more explicit,' he began gravely, and there was now no latent sarcasm in his manner. After all, these vague remarks might point to some real perplexity; she might be in difficulty herself; she might even need a friend.

'That is exactly what I cannot be,' she replied quickly, and then she hesitated.

Why was she so anxious to know this man's opinion? A week ago he had been a stranger to her, and even now she knew little about him; but there was something about Dr. Lyall, a certain quiet strength and self-reliance, that made people willing to trust him. No man had ever had more secrets confided to him—women especially told him their troubles—for one thing he was never afraid of speaking the truth to them.

Gerda was vaguely sensible of all this. Dr. Lyall was different from most men; he was less selfish and less self-engrossed. In his busy life he had still leisure to interest himself in other people. Could she not obtain his unprejudiced opinion in some roundabout way? It would be impossible to speak plainly; but she might draw an imaginary case.

'Suppose, for the sake of argument,' she began, 'that a girl found herself in a difficult position; that all her friends had agreed to put a pressure on her to do a certain thing, and that to please them and make them happy she must do it or else bring herself into trouble with them. Of course,' breaking off hastily, 'I am only quoting this as an example to illustrate my theory—that girls are too much coerced.'

'Oh, of course I understand that;' but Dr. Lyall gave his companion a quick glance as he said this. 'May I venture to ask if this supposititious young lady were unwilling to fall in with her friends' views?'

'We will say she was not willing—or, perhaps, to render it a little more complex, we will put it that she was hardly sure in her own mind whether she wished it or not. Anyhow, this free agent, as you call her, would be subjected to daily and hourly pressure.'

'I begin to see what you mean,' he returned slowly, as though he were pondering every word. 'If there were many similar cases you would be certainly right in saying men have the best of it. But, Miss Meredith, after all, it is perfectly simple for women as well as for men—there can be but one right and wrong; surely we have not one code for the male and another for the female sex.'

'Certainly not.'

'This fictitious young lady may have a great deal to bear from her friends' importunity—I will not deny that—but no coercion, no well-meant advice, ought to prevail with her against her conscience. If my sister were to come and ask me: "Shall I do this or that thing?—take care how you answer me, for it will involve the happiness or unhappiness of my life"—I would not be so presumptuous as to answer her. Why should I direct another human being's life? I might, indeed, offer her advice, I might point out the pitfalls that would lie in her way; but the decision would rest with her. Follow your conscience, do what you think would be right and true, and leave the results.'

'Thank you!' For the moment Gerda felt she could say no more; but, to her surprise, Dr. Lyall went on talking:

'It is very strange that we should have had this argument, for I was once placed myself in this painful position. Perhaps you do not know that I have another sister beside Pamela?'

'Miss Lyall told me about her—she is married.'

'Yes; that is the unfortunate part of it. She has married the wrong man. But she would not allow that he was anything but the right one—though we both tried, Pamela and I, to prove to her her mistake. Hester is two years older than I am, and a very clever woman. Her husband ought to have been superior to herself, or at least her equal—it was degrading her intellect to marry Julius Vincent.'

'What is wrong with him?'

'What is right with him? you might say. Oh, you need not be shocked—my brother-in law has no vices: he is simply an idle, an irresponsible being, who has not arrived at his full stature.'

'And yet your sister loved him?'

'I suppose so. Julius contrived to win her affections; ladies call him fascinating. Well, Miss Meredith, now for my difficulty: my sister came to me and said, in so many words, "I love this man; I never intend to marry anyone else. I would rather be unhappy with him than live without him: if I do not become his wife my life will be spoilt; but I will not marry him if you forbid me to do so."'

'Did she really say that?'

'She did—and, what is more, she would have abided by her words: my sister is a conscientious woman. She had heard all my arguments before; there was no use in my repeating them. I had told her before that if she married Julius Vincent she would be a needy woman all her life; but when she put it to me like this, when she insisted on making me, her brother, the arbitrator of her fate, I refused to speak. I would not forbid her to marry him.'

'I think you were right—and, in any case, she knew your opinion.'

'She knew it. And three weeks afterwards she married him, and my words have come true. Julius does not work; he paints bad pictures, and wastes his time and strength. Hester keeps a day-school, that she and her children may have bread enough to eat and to keep their heads out of debt. Why do I tell you this painful story, Miss Meredith? Is it not to illustrate my theory—as you have yours—that we must do what we think right, even if it give us pain and leave results. Forgive me for preaching such a sermon,' with a short laugh, 'but you have brought it on yourself.'

'I have nothing to forgive; on the contrary, I am extremely obliged to you. Dr. Lyall!'—suddenly—'I have no idea where we are, and it is growing dark.'

'I was about to observe the same thing. We are on the highroad to Chilverton, and we have turned once: the sign-post told me as much five minutes ago.'

'Have we passed the sign-post?' in a relieved tone. 'Then we have only to turn down Bramble Lane, as it is called, and there is a short-cut that will bring us to the Hall in ten minutes.'

'Then by all means let us take it, before it gets too dark to see our way—for it is quite time for you to be home. This is the result of getting too deeply into argument. I had not the slightest intention of giving you more than ten minutes of my company. I think I must apologize to Mrs. Meredith. Shall I?'

Gerda made no objection, and they both quickened their steps, and in a few more minutes they were at their destination.

Mrs. Meredith received the doctor's excuses very graciously. Gerda had a bad habit, she said, of going out between lights. In the village it did not matter, everyone knew them; but the roads were certainly very lonely. She must forbid such walks in the future; her girls were too fearless and independent. She was much obliged to Dr. Lyall for his escort, and she could not see that he was to blame for so kindly taking care of her daughter.

Dr. Lyall was exonerated, but Gerda herself did not escape scot-free. Her mother followed her to her room.

'This must never happen again, Gerda,'

she said with rather a grave face. You are too incautious, my dear. I am sure Gerard would object to you walking with Dr. Lyall. Of course,' as Gerda looked vexed at this allusion to her cousin, ' I see exactly how it happened. He was coming out of Braeside, and, as he was walking in the same direction, he joined you.'

'Yes, and then we got into an argument, and walked a little too far.'

'Just so. Well, for this once I will excuse it; but, as I said before, it must never occur again. For the future you must take your walks earlier, and there is no need for you to go alone either. Doris or I can accompany you. You are too independent, Gerda, and, after all, you are only a very young lady.'

'Very well, mother; I will be more careful for the future;' and Gerda sealed this promise with a penitent kiss.

Mrs. Meredith so seldom asserted her authority, that this unusual and dignified remonstrance had its desired effect, and nothing would have induced Gerda to allow Dr. Lyall to walk many yards with her again along the Chesterton roads.

CHAPTER X.

AN INNOCENT MATCHMAKER.

'True friendship can afford true knowledge. It does not depend on darkness or ignorance.'—THOREAU.

GERDA had received her mother's rebuke very sweetly, but she would have been both surprised and grieved if she had guessed how severely Dr. Lyall had taken himself to task for his incautiousness.

'What right have I to be running after that girl?' he said to himself, as he walked back to Braeside. 'What right have I to let her see—as she must see—the pleasure I take in her society, just because she is simpler and more genuine than other girls? Perhaps, after all'—with momentary wavering—'it does not matter to a tough old fellow like me. At thirty-two one is no boy, and a passing fancy cannot hurt me. It is not likely that I should have made an impression on her. 'What a child she is,' he went on, after following this line of thought for a few minutes, ' in spite of her clever talk! She had no idea how thoroughly I understood her vague illustration. Poor little girl! So they are all bent on marrying her to the handsome cousin, and, from the little I have seen, the young fellow wishes it too. Well, he is a fine, manly type of a young Englishman, and I do not believe she could do better for herself than take him. If I know anything about human nature, he is a thoroughly good fellow. So she is not quite ready with her yea, yea—that is so like a woman. She fears to cheapen herself by too speedy an assent. In this sort of case, to waver is to yield. I expect Hamlyn will get his way sooner or later. "This lady doth protest too much." And yet the poor child seemed terribly in earnest.'

Human nature is somewhat complex in its workings. For some reason best known to himself, Dr. Lyall was anxious to prove to himself most clearly that Miss Meredith's vacillation of purpose, her doubts and tremors, all showed that she was really not so averse to the family plan, after all.

'She is more sensitive than most girls,' he continued. 'Her conscience is over-scrupulous, and she has a fine notion of honour—this does her credit. By-and-by her scruples will adjust themselves. One day she will wake up to the consciousness that sentiment and duty are reconciled, and then she will accept him all the more thankfully that she has undergone a martyrdom in his behalf. I suppose I am an old fool—I decline to call myself a young one—but I think Hamlyn is to be envied. It must be rather pleasant to have a superior woman concentrating all her thoughts on one in that intelligent fashion. The generality of girls I have seen are certainly feebler in mind, and as a rule they do not interest me. Heigho! One must not pay too dearly for a week's idleness. I will go and have a game of billiards with Hake before dinner. That will be a wiser plan than indulging in introspection.'

Dr. Lyall carried out this resolution promptly. He had a thoroughly healthy organization of mind and body, a steady temperament that would carry him safely through perils to which weaker men would at once succumb. He was sharp-sighted enough to see the danger that menaced him. He was on the brink; he must be wary and draw back in time, before he was wholly fascinated. Dr. Lyall's hand was as steady as usual that evening. He won every game, much to his friend's chagrin, and at dinner he was unusually pugnacious, for he inveigled the curate, Mr. Allingham, into an argument, and vanquished him in every point.

'Lyall is in force to-night,' observed Captain Hake when they left the table. 'He has left Allingham without a leg to stand on.'

Gerda would have been thankful for a quiet half-hour after her mother had left her; she wanted to review her conversation with Dr. Lyall. But she wasn't to be left in peace. Before ten minutes passed, Doris burst into the room.

'They have come, Gerda; they drove up in the waggonette five minutes ago. You never saw such a lot of men, and most of them tall. Let me see, there was Captain Drummond, and Mr. Harry Power and his brother, and Mr. Seymour and Mr. Lorraine, and his cousin, Fulbert Stanley, and—oh, I forget his name—the dark man with the hook nose, who gave you the petunias.'

'I suppose you mean Mr. Unwin?'

'Yes, of course. I wish his nose was not so excessively Jewish; but he is not really bad-looking. Now, Gerda, we must fly, and dress ourselves, for mother does look so nervous. Gerard is showing them their rooms. Do you hear them tramping down the gallery? I am so excited that I shall never be ready. Mind you put on your dark-blue velveteen, Gerda, for you look so sweet in that. Do hurry up, as Gerard says;' and with this parting monition Doris disappeared.

Gerda heaved an impatient sigh, but her sense of duty made her dress rapidly and hasten to her mother's side. Her manners were so winning and gracious as she received Gerard's friends, that the young man felt a thrill of pride as he watched her.

'She is a darling,' he said to himself. 'I can see how all those fellows admire her. What a wife she will make for me one of these days, if only I can get her to say "Yes!"'

Honest Gerard was becoming thoroughly in earnest, whatever Gerda might choose to aver to the contrary. Propinquity had done much for him. His good-humoured acquiescence in Sir Godfrey's scheme had yielded to a real desire to win his cousin ; and more than once on this evening Gerda detected him looking at her with unusual seriousness in his eyes.

The dinner-table that night was a merry one. Sir Godfrey told one or two of his favourite stories, which were listened to by the young men with due respect and decorum. Mr. Seymour, indeed, who had heard them before, was a little too ready with his laugh before the proper tickling point had been reached, but Sir Godfrey benevolently overlooked this.

'You will laugh more before I finish,' he said benignly. And he was right, for long before the climax was reached Mr. Seymour's suppressed mirth had broken all bounds, and had communicated its infection to the other young men.

'Gentlemen, gentlemen! pray allow me to finish,' pleaded poor Sir Godfrey ; but he was not permitted to do so, though this was the best story of all—his *bonne bouche.*

'It is of no use, Sir Godfrey. You have nearly killed us already ; you should be more careful, really. Look at Drummond ; how red in the face he is, and apoplexy in his family, too! Apoplexy—or insanity, which is it, Drummond? I am never quite sure,' continued the lively youth.

Sir Godfrey gave one of his old-fashioned little bows. He hardly knew whether to regard Mr. Seymour's hilarity as a compliment or not; he never liked to be interrupted in his stories, especially that story, and yet, how was it possible to proceed amid peals of laughter?

'If you say any more, Sir Godfrey, our deaths will lie at your door. It is exquisite cruelty, is it not, Drummond? to ask a man to eat such a dinner as this, and then threaten him with apoplexy, by telling him such a story.' And Mr. Seymour shook his head sadly at the old gentleman.

'Shut up, you fool!' whispered Gerard savagely in his chum's ear. 'He will see you are poking fun at him directly.'

But Sir Godfrey saw nothing of the kind. Charlie Seymour was a special favourite, and had his privileges; and, like a wise youth, he always knew the length of his tether, so he at once began talking across the table to Gerda on esoteric Buddhism.

'You are a pupil of occultism, I know, Miss Meredith, and are a devout follower of Madame Blavatsky, and the Arkats and Mahatmas, commonly known as the Brothers. I suppose by this time you have gained additional knowledge; I am rather anxious about my Karma.'

'I am sorry that I cannot give you any information, Mr. Seymour,' returned Gerda sweetly; 'I had no idea you took interest in esoteric science. This is quite a new departure, is it not? Mother, do you not think it is time for us to go? I expect Grand has another story ready;' and at this very broad hint Mrs. Meredith rose at once.

Charlie Seymour was an old adversary, and he and Gerda never met without one pitched battle at least. He had a knack of drawing her out on one of her pet hobbies—Buddhism, Comparative Mythology or Psychology, it did not matter what; and when she had waxed warm and eloquent, and had sufficiently displayed her partial knowledge or utter ignorance, he would then and there turn the whole subject into fun. But for once Gerda was wary, and refused to be entrapped into a discussion.

'I am so glad you remember what you read, Mr. Seymour,' she said, sending a Parthian arrow as she swept out of the room.

The evening passed very pleasantly. Two or three of the guests were decidedly musical: Mr. Harry Power had brought his violin, and his brother played the clarionet; Captain Drummond and the irrepressible Charlie Seymour had good voices; and as both Gerda and Doris sung, they had quite a musical entertainment, which lasted until Sir Godfrey woke up from his usual evening nap, and rather peremptorily ordered all the men off to the billiard-room.

Neither did the next few hours hang heavily on their hands. A brisk six miles walk, a good deal of exercise in the winter tennis-court, and two or three games at billiards after tea, filled up the day. The girls had joined in the tennis tournament, but Mrs. Meredith would not hear of their accompanying the walking party, though Mrs. Hake would willingly have chaperoned them, as she and the Lyalls were to walk with the gentlemen. But they were not without female companionship, as Charlie Seymour expressed it, for as they passed the vicarage they encountered the two Hilton girls and Robina Stewart, with two of the Stewart lads and Mr. Allingham as escort, and Mrs. Hake had induced them to accompany the walking party.

Gerda felt a little pang of regret when Robina told her all about it afterwards. She would have liked to have been of the party, but her mother needed her help, and both she and Doris were kept busy until tea-time. An hour later, as Doris was passing through the hall on her way from the drawing-room, she saw Gerard standing on the bearskin rug, staring rather gloomily into the fire.

'I thought you were playing billiards, Gerard,' she observed, with some surprise.

'No; I was only looking on; the other fellows are having a match. Where is Gerda? Not dressing already?'—as Doris pointed to the staircase.

'Well, I believe so. Mother told us that we were to be very punctual; but all the same I don't mean to move for another half-hour. That is the best of having a curly crop'—passing her hand over the mass of short soft curls, that somehow suited her face. 'If I had Gerda's long hair I should take ever so much more time to dress.'

'Yes, of course.' But it was easy to see that Gerard had not heard a word of this. He was pulling his moustaches in a perturbed manner, and there was an anxious frown on his brow. 'Look here, Doris,' he said suddenly, 'you and I have always been chums, and I am going to have the first dance with you to-night.'

'Oh, not really, Gerard!' and Doris blushed very prettily at this unexpected compliment.

'So you are engaged to me, you see. Well, we have settled that, and now I want to speak to you about something else. Do you think'—clearing his voice—'that I have a grain of chance with Gerda?'

Doris started, and the pretty colour left her cheeks a little suddenly. She was deep in Gerard's confidence; she had found out all about it one day when they two were having a long walk together, and she had given him a great deal of support and sympathy in her girlish way, and it was understood between them that on all possible and impossible occasions she was to advance Gerard's cause.

'You see,' he went on, for Doris was only twisting her fingers nervously together, and had not answered, 'Uncle Godfrey has been prodding me on again—not that I require prodding'—becoming suddenly conscious that this form of expression was not exactly suitable to the circumstances. 'Uncle Godfrey is always in such a hurry—"Why not do it to-night?" he said to me an hour ago; "you could not have a better opportunity. I have my reasons for giving you this bit of advice, and I assure you you won't repent taking it." Now, what on earth did he mean by that?'

'I am sure I do not know,' returned Doris, shaking her head rather dejectedly; 'but you need not do it all the same, Gerard; it would be the worst possible time to choose. You and Gerda ought to be thinking only of your guests; not—not——' But here Doris stammered and broke down. 'She—she would not like it, you know.'

'Why not?' for this opposition spurred him on afresh. 'Lots of fellows do it at balls; the music and crowd help, somehow. You don't see the difficulty, Doris'—taking her arm and marching her up and down the polished floor. 'I never can get Gerda alone for a minute. She refuses to walk with me unless you accompany us, and if I ever catch her alone she makes some excuse to leave me. I told you all this before, and you promised to help me'—a little reproachfully.

'So I will, Gerard'—with a suspicious catch in her breath. 'I always—always want to help you.'

'Yes, I know you are a dear little soul, Doey'—Gerard's pet name for her—'and I am not blaming you the least; but I am a bit down about it to-night. I sometimes think she will not have anything to say to me, because I do not care for her books.'

'But you do read sometimes, Gerard.'

'Yes, the paper—and I don't mind a novel, if there is any go in it; but'—with a trace of contempt in his tone for Doris's slowness of comprehension—'do you call that reading? Gerda would like me to study Carlyle and Emerson and Ruskin, and all the old literary fogies, and then she would expect me to talk about them.'

'But surely all that is not necessary in—in—— You know what I mean, Gerard;' for the magnitude of the subject overwhelmed Doris.

'You mean that it is not a necessary condition, or even corollary, of the marriage service. Well, I suppose not, if only Gerda can be persuaded of the fact. I would not allow it to anyone else, but she is just a little bit too uppish on these subjects; for all her grand talk, it is not necessary for a man to be a book-worm. If I can only prove this to her!'

'You must try, Gerard, but I would not— I would not do it to-night if I were you. Now I must really go. Please, please, do not keep me a moment longer, or mother will be annoyed;' and then Gerard reluctantly let her go.

There were two little pearly drops on Doris's hot cheeks as she stood before her toilet-table.

'He is wrong; he must be wrong,' she sighed. 'Gerda could never find it in her heart to refuse him; she is only just keeping him in suspense. I wish he would not be so worried; he was not a bit like himself to-night. Of course she will say "Yes" to him: she shall, she must. It would be too dreadful to see Gerard unhappy.'

'We must do what we think right, even if it give us pain, and leave results,' Gerda was saying to herself that moment. 'How clearly he put it—it was like a sudden flash of strong light in some dark place, it seemed to illumine everything. I must remember those words if I ever find myself in a difficulty again. He is very wise. I should think he made fewer mistakes than most people. Oh, if one could have such a friend!' and Gerda echoed Doris's sigh.

CHAPTER XI.

GERARD FINDS HIS OPPORTUNITY.

'Most men find they have more courage than they themselves think they have.'—GREVILLE.

MRS. HAKE had made a solemn covenant and promise that she and her guests would be the first to arrive on the eventful evening. She had yielded most willingly to Doris's entreaties to this effect, and had endorsed them for the benefit of Mrs. Meredith, who was a little overwhelmed by her responsibilities.

'We must insist on the Braeside people coming punctually,' Doris had said a few evenings previously. 'There can be no stiffness or formality when Mrs. Hake is in the room; she will make us begin dancing at once, instead of standing about looking at each other;' for Doris was determined to extract as much enjoyment as possible from her first grown-up party.

Mrs. Hake was a woman of honour, and she kept her word; she hunted up her husband and Dr. Lyall from their cosy arm-chairs in the study, and she hurried Pamela remorselessly over her toilet, though that self-willed young lady disliked to hurry herself, and she marshalled her forces with such tact and diplomacy that Captain Hake forgot to grumble, and they were actually at the door of Chesterton Hall before the clock struck eight.

As they passed round the heavy-carved screen that shut off the entrance-door, the ladies uttered an exclamation of delighted surprise; indeed, Pamela thought it was the most picturesque scene she had ever beheld. All the furniture had been moved into corners or taken away, and the grand proportions of the fine old hall were fully seen for the first time. The Japanese screen had been withdrawn, and the wide broad staircase was exposed to view, the crimson carpet, and pots of azaleas, and tall leafy ferns adding to the effect. A single row of oil-lamps ran round the gallery, while numberless lights below gleamed among wreaths of evergreens and drooping flags. Mrs. Meredith and her daughters stood among the group of gentlemen on the rug. The girls were dressed alike in soft white silk gowns, only Gerda had a spray of pale pink flowers. They had just finished dressing, when their mother had summoned them mysteriously to their grandfather's dressing-room. They found Sir Godfrey standing before an Indian cabinet; he had two worn morocco cases in his hand.

'Gerda,' he said, with his usual solemnity, 'you are the elder, and must have the first choice; take whichever you like, my dear, and my little Dorrie shall have the other.'

Gerda opened the cases; the first one contained a gold necklace of fine antique work, with a pendant of small rose diamonds; in the other there was a double row of pearls with a tiny invisible clasp. The pearls were not large, but their whiteness and delicacy took Gerda's fancy.

'I would rather have the pearls, Grand,' she said, in a satisfied tone; and Sir Godfrey himself clasped the dainty necklace round Gerda's full white throat.

'The children look very nice to-night, Honoria,' he observed, when he had dismissed them; 'neither of them are handsome; but Doris has youth and health, and Gerda is as graceful as a young fawn. I like to see a girl carry her head well.' But here Sir Godfrey checked himself with a short sigh, as he remembered the last time there had been a ball in the old Hall, when Clare and Honoria were girls, and how the slim, dark-eyed Clare had been the belle of the evening.

Mrs. Meredith drew her lace shawl round her shoulders with a slight movement of impatience. Her girls were beautiful in her eyes, and she was dissatisfied with her father's qualified praise. She thought Gerda was looking positively lovely to-night; the pale waxy flowers—Gerard's gift—had given her the touch of colour she needed; there was a soft brightness in her eyes, and the faintest rose tint in her cheeks. Mrs. Meredith's maternal vanity would have been gratified if she had only known how thoroughly Gerard and Dr. Lyall shared her opinion.

As the Braeside party joined the group

round the fire, they found Gerda laying down the law with the utmost animation to Captain Drummond and two or three of the other gentlemen, while Doris listened with a perplexed face.

'It is not right,' she was saying, in her clear young voice. 'Do not let Mr. Seymour talk you over, Dorrie; it is not fair on the other girls; it is taking a mean advantage of them.—Don't you agree with me, Dr. Lyall?'—as he advanced towards the circle —'is it right for us, the daughters of the house, to fill up our programmes before our guests arrive? Doris's programme is full, and I want her to burn it.'

'But surely you mean to dance yourself, Miss Meredith?'

Gerard answered for her:

'She is going to give me three valses, I know. After that it does not matter to me when you fellows cut in.'

'Gerard, be quiet! I will promise you nothing until the other girls have their programmes filled, and then I will dance with everybody.'

'Don't listen to her, Miss Doris,' whispered Charlie Seymour; 'keep your programme—or, look here: let me keep it for you;' and he took it out of Doris's unresisting hand.

Doris looked after it regretfully; she had herself written that shaky 'G. H.' against the first dance, and had explained to each gentleman in succession that the initials belonged to her cousin Gerard. This was the crowning glory of the evening to Doris—this first valse with Gerard. When the moment drew near and the music began, she dimpled with such pride and pleasure that more than one pair of eyes followed her with amused admiration, and Gerard himself looked at her very kindly.

'How grand you look to-night, Doey! Diamonds, too!' with a glance at the glittering pendant. 'Come along, we shall have the floor to ourselves;' and Gerard's strong arm and smooth step transported the little girl into a sort of Elysium.

That no one could dance like Gerard was part of Doris's creed, and even Gerda agreed that it was the one thing he did perfectly.

Sir Godfrey was afraid he was growing just a little deaf; he said as much to Charlie Seymour.

'I am afraid I am getting a little hard of hearing, as our Stokes says,' he observed. 'I thought I overheard Dalton telling the Hiltons' coachman to bring round the carriage at half-past two—but of course it must have been my fancy: half-past twelve were my orders.'

'I am afraid there must be a draught somewhere,' returned Charlie nonchalantly. 'If you take my advice, Sir Godfrey, you will keep at the other end of the hall; there! I hear wheels; the door is going to open again. My dear sir, I positively insist on your taking more care of yourself.' And Charlie took his host's arm, and forcibly conducted him to the fireplace.

'What an extraordinary thing! Grandfather's clock has stopped!' observed Gerard gravely, as he carried off Gerda for the second valse.

Gerda stood still in amazement.

'What can have happened to it?' she asked anxiously. But a sudden twinkle in Gerard's eyes undeceived her.

'You must ask Seymour. I am afraid that bad boy has been up to his tricks again. "Small and early"—that is a comprehensive term, he assures me. Happily, the roads are safe, and there is some chance of a moon.'

'You two have been plotting mischief,' returned Gerda shrewdly. 'Grand thinks it will be all over at half-past twelve. I heard him tell Mrs. Owen that he considered these Cinderella dances so sensible. He will be very angry when he finds it out, Gerard.'

'We will make up a rubber of whist presently, and then he will know nothing about it. I think this is going to be a success, Gerda; the people all seem enjoying themselves. Look at Allingham! That is the second time he has danced with the fair Frances. I wonder what his Vicar would say?'

Mr. Allingham had forgotten all about his Vicar. Frances Hilton always looked back on the evening of the Hamlyns' dance as one of the most important crises of her life, for it was in the dimly-lighted conservatory that Herbert Allingham had ventured to speak of his love. 'Lots of fellows do it at balls,' Gerard had said, and on this evening his words were verified.

'Do you intend to spare me one dance?' asked Dr. Lyall, as Gerard deposited his cousin on a seat, and rushed off to secure his next partner; and as he asked the question he took the fan out of her hand, and began to fan her with a practised hand.

Gerda elevated her eyebrows slightly.

'I thought you did not care about dancing?'

'Oh, there are exceptions to every rule; and I shall care very much about dancing with you. I am afraid, though, that I shall hardly distinguish myself as creditably as Hamlyn—he seems an exceptionally good dancer.'

'So we all think. Gerard is quite in his element to-night. What do you think, Dr. Lyall? He and Mr. Seymour have stopped grandfather's clock for fear of its telling tales, and they have given orders to Dalton that none of the carriages are to come until half-past two. Grand would be in such a fuss if he knew that. Are you ready?' as Dr. Lyall smiled and offered his arm, and she rose a little reluctantly.

She did not quite believe in Dr. Lyall's capabilities as a partner, and she would rather have talked to him in this quiet corner. She was agreeably surprised, however. Dr. Lyall did not acquit himself so badly, after all. He had a good ear, and danced quietly and evenly.

'I think you were hardly speaking the truth when you said you could not dance,' Gerda observed rather reproachfully as they paced up and down the long gallery, which was used to-night as a promenade. Pamela flashed an amused look at them as she passed.

Alick was looking quite young and good-looking, she thought; evening dress always suited dark men. He made an excellent foil to Miss Meredith's fairness; she, too, was looking unusually well—that coronet of plaits just suited her style. She had a faint idea that Alick rather admired her; though she dare not hint such a thing to him for worlds, for, with all her audacity, Pamela was a little in awe of her brother.

'Did I say I could not dance?' remonstrated Dr. Lyall. 'I think you must have misunderstood me. I am rather indifferent on the subject; but, after all, it is good exercise.'

Dr. Lyall spoke in an easy, unembarrassed tone, but he was secretly conscious of an undue bounding of his pulses at this implied compliment. He was a fool, of course—he was always calling himself a fool now—but it was very pleasant sauntering up and down with a certain little gloved hand resting on his arm.

'Do you admire our decorations?' she asked next.

'Very much,' was the reply; 'but you must forgive me if I say the light is a little too subdued. So much black oak absorbs the brightness of all those lamps. If you could only have electric light, now, the effect would be superb.'

'I suppose so. That is the worst of you Londoners—nothing is good enough for you. To our country-bred minds this soft moony light is very pretty.'

'Did I say otherwise? You are a little hard on me to-night, Miss Meredith. But perhaps I expressed myself awkwardly. I know when I go back to town I shall carry away a vivid picture of this old hall. Can anything be prettier than that moving crowd below us—all those smiling faces and gay dresses?'

'There is Captain Drummond looking up

at us. I am engaged to him for the next dance. You are not going back to town yet, Dr. Lyall? you have only been here a week.'

'It has been the longest week I have ever spent in my life, and I think I may say the pleasantest,' responded Dr. Lyall a little dreamily. 'Yes, we leave the day after to-morrow; my patients cannot spare me any longer. Besides, ten days' idleness is enough for any man.'

'That is very soon,' replied Gerda in a low voice.

And then Captain Drummond came up to them and carried her off. Gerda did not make herself as pleasant as usual to her partner. She was a little absent and *distraite*. She was sorry to hear that the Lyalls were leaving so soon. She liked Pamela, and wanted to know her better, and she was by no means indifferent to Pamela's brother.

'What is the use of making friends if one has to lose them?' she thought discontentedly. 'When Dr. Lyall gets back to his patients, he will forget all about us. I dare say he will not even remember that he has saved my life, though I shall never, never forget it.'

Gerard had not found his opportunity yet.

He had had his three valses with Gerda, in spite of all her protestations.

'You ought not to monopolize me to-night,' she said in rather a vexed voice, as he came up to her the third time ; 'besides, I am sure that this dance belongs to Mr. Seymour.'

'I will make it right with him,' returned Gerard easily. 'You ought to be grateful to me for rescuing you from a partner who only reaches your shoulder. I do hate to see a tall girl and a little man dancing together. You and Seymour look like a wasp and a may-pole together. You need not dance with me, you know, and we can sit out if you like.'

But Gerda could not be induced to see this. She liked dancing with Gerard better than with anyone, and she knew that when they danced together people stood still to watch them. Her step suited his perfectly, so it was no wonder that, as Dr. Lyall looked down on them from the gallery, he muttered to himself that it was the perfect poetry of motion.

'Is not this a charming scene, Alick ?' and Pamela roused him with a smart tap of her fan. 'Are you watching the dancers ? Does not Mr. Hamlyn waltz well ? He has only asked me once, and that is the third time he has danced with his cousin.'

'Do you mean that you are envious, Pam? I thought Vincent objected to valses.' And Dr. Lyall looked at his sister with latent fun in his eyes.

Pamela frowned. Evidently the remark did not please her.

'I hope you do not expect me to give in to all Derrick's absurd views. When he gives up smoking I will promise to give up dancing. I mean to tell him that some day; that is the worst of being engaged'—and Pamela looked very pretty and naughty—'it is putting yourself in the power of a tyrant. Derrick thinks he has the right to lecture me.'

'Well, I suppose he has—at least, he believes he has the right. But when you talk of tyranny, I think it is rather the other way. I don't think Vincent gets the best of it.'

'Oh, I am quite aware of your opinion by this time,' returned Pamela, with a vixenish look at her brother's amused face. 'Why do you not go and tell Derrick all my faults, and beg him to give me up? It would be so like you, Alick, to go and do a thing of that kind, and call it duty.'

'Would it? Do you know, I expect he has found them all out by this time. In spite of his laziness, Vincent is very shrewd and clear-sighted. I dare say you often give him a taste of your temper, Pam.'

'Oh, you are not going to exasperate me,' she replied quickly. 'Why do you not go and dance, instead of finding fault with your poor little sister? There is that plain Miss Hilton without a partner—let me introduce you to her.'

'Thanks, awfully; but I have finished dancing for to-night. You had better talk to her instead.'

But Pamela only shrugged her shoulders. In another minute the yellowish silk skirt was floating away among the dancers. Pamela had no moments to throw away on plain-faced Augusta Hilton. The irrepressible Charlie had consoled himself for his lost partner in listening to her sharp, merry speeches.

'She is engaged, is she?' Charlie was heard to remark later on in the smoking-room. 'Who's the fellow? I have half a mind to call him out. Six feet high, is he?'—in answer to some remark—'well, I don't care. David stood up to Goliath, didn't he? and your humble servant has cheek enough for anything. I like a lively girl with plenty of go in her. Temper! Of course she has got a temper. All the right sort of women have—prevents stagnation, wholesome irritant, and all that kind of thing. If it were not for Goliath I would go in and win.'

'Is it Miss Lyall's charms or the champagne that has been too much for you, Charlie?' asked Captain Drummond lazily. 'Take my advice, my dear boy—"marry with your ears, and not with your eyes." Miss Lyall's voice is not to my taste; it is a trifle too acrid.'

Gerard had not yet found his opportunity. It was growing late—a fact of which Sir Godfrey was happily oblivious; he and his partner had just won their second rubber, and the third was inevitable. But all comes to him who waits, and just then a set of lancers was formed, and Gerda relinquished her partner under the plea of fatigue to the younger Miss Hilton. Gerard, who was also resting from his labours, strolled quietly across the hall, and joined her.

'We are both out of it, I see,' he observed as she gave him a welcoming smile. 'Suppose we find a quiet corner somewhere;' and Gerda fell innocently into the trap.

She was a little surprised, however, when Gerard led the way to the morning-room. It had not been used that evening, and the fire had burnt low. Gerard took up the poker and stirred it a little noisily, while Gerda stood beside him on the rug. The next moment he threw it down, and took hold of her hands.

'Gerda, I want to speak to you—it is no good putting it off any longer. Do you remember that question I asked you in the boat last spring?' Then she tried to shrink away from him, but his grasp was too strong. 'I told you then that I should try again,' he went on, 'and I meant it. You were very hard on me that day, you would not believe that I was in earnest; but I meant it then, and I mean it a hundred times more now. You will give me a different answer now, dear, will you not?'

'Oh, Gerard, not to-night! Please do not ask me to-night;' and there was such a troubled look on her face that he released her hand, and an anxious expression came into his eyes.

'I have given you plenty of time to think of it,' he returned reproachfully. 'Nine months—that is surely long enough! You could not have misunderstood me, Gerda. I was always fond of you, but now I would rather have you for my wife than any other girl. You believe that, do you not?'—speaking very gravely. 'If you will only consent to marry me, you shall never repent it—never.'

'Gerard, I cannot—do not ask me!' and Gerda sank into a seat and covered her face with her hands. What were those words that seemed to surge through her brain over and over again? 'We must do what we think right, even if it give us pain, and leave results. We must do what we think right.' 'I cannot—indeed I cannot!'

'But why not?' he pleaded, and his face became a little pale. 'We have always been such friends, you and I. I know you are fond of me, Gerda—you cannot deny that; and if it's not quite the right feeling, if it has not grown with you as it has with me, it will come, if you are only patient.'

But he seemed speaking to deaf ears. An inner voice was clamouring to be heard too, and would not be silenced: 'Follow your conscience; do what you think to be right and true.'

'Gerard, I dare not do it. It would be wrong to you as well as to myself. I love you, but not in that way;' and the agonized sincerity of her voice struck a chill into Gerard's heart. But he would not be baffled yet. This was his last chance, and he must make the most of it.

'You think that you do not care for me enough,' he replied gently. 'But suppose I am willing to take the risk of that, and to be content with what you have to give me?'

But she shook her head sadly.

'Nothing would make it right. I am very sorry, Gerard, but you must give it up. I would do anything for you but this. I would die for you if need be'—with a quick, loving impulse that she could not resist. But he only answered this by a melancholy smile.

'I would rather you lived for me. Gerda, just be patient with me another minute. I want to get to the bottom of this. Are you afraid that I shall not satisfy you? Are you giving me this answer because I do not care for all the books and things for which you care? Is it because you think I am not clever enough? I cannot promise to alter— a man must act up to his own nature—but you will be making a grievous mistake if you let this come between us.'

'Oh, Gerard, it is not that;' and for the moment Gerda thought she was speaking the truth.

'Then what is it? But there, I will not press you. I always knew you were too good for me, Gerda. I was a fool not to see there was no chance for me.'

'I wish I could have answered differently,' she sighed. 'But you will not think me too unkind, will you? If you only knew how unhappy you have made me, I am sure you would forgive me.'

'There is nothing to forgive,' he returned hastily. 'I have tried and failed. It is no fault of yours if you cannot make up your mind to take me. Look here, Gerda, I have said my last word; I would not be such a cad as to persecute you. You have nothing more to fear from me. I shall be Cousin Gerard to the end of the chapter.'

She bent her head in answer to this, but he could see the slow tears rolling down her cheeks. How good he was! how manly and generous! How could she find it in her heart to say him nay?

'I don't want you to fret about it. I suppose I shall get over it some day—other fellows do. Now I may as well go back to my duties;' and as she did not look up or make any response, he bent over her and kissed the coronet of soft shining hair. It was the first time he had ever kissed her, and he knew it would be the last. But Gerda was hardly conscious of the act as she wiped the tears away with her handkerchief. It was the first real pain in her young life, and she felt as though she hardly knew how to bear it.

CHAPTER XII.

'YOU HAVE HELPED ME.'

'When you are young grief is a tempest which prostrates you; at mature age it is simply a north wind which adds a wrinkle to your brow and one more white hair to your head.'
— *Thoughts of a Queen.*

IT was nearly three o'clock, and more than one carriage had driven away with its merry chattering occupants, when Dr. Lyall, straying through the deserted rooms in search of his hostess, wandered into the morning-room, attracted by the cheery blaze of the renovated fire. Charlie Seymour was rattling off a lively valse, while the musicians were refreshing themselves, and the indefatigable Pamela was whirling away with Captain Drummond. The other couples had followed her example, Doris and Gerard among them; for Gerard, in spite of the dull gnawing pain at his heart, could not resist Doris's plaintive and appealing blue eyes. 'Please dance with me,' they seemed to say, and with his customary good-nature he had given in. But after all, Doris was not to enjoy her dance; the first two rounds were perfect, and then she had whispered breathlessly:

'I saw you with Gerda just now. Did you do it, Gerard?' But Gerard tightened his grasp a little convulsively; he had not expected this.

'Hush! don't ask me, Doey. There is no chance for me now. I wish I had taken your advice; but one cannot always be wise. Never speak of it again, there's a good girl!' and Gerard's step became so rapid that Doris turned a little giddy.

'I think I will sit down,' she faltered; 'I am so sorry, Gerard. It was good of you to dance with me!' and then she moved away from him, and sat down with a very sober face.

Poor Doris! it was hard on her—on her first party, too. 'She has hurt him—oh, she has hurt him dreadfully!' she thought; and her bosom heaved with indignant sympathy.

Dr. Lyall had caught the gleam of a white

dress in the firelight, and his eyes brightened a little; but the next moment he was conscious of a revulsion of feeling. At the sound of his step Gerda had looked up at him, and her eyes were still full of tears. Her paleness and intense agitation were so apparent that, after the first impulse to withdraw, his professional instinct drew him towards her.

'You are not well; you have fatigued yourself. Let me fetch you a glass of wine?' But she put out a cold shaking hand to stop him.

'No, thank you, I do not want anything; I am only a little troubled about something that has happened. It is foolish to cry,' as a large tear fell in her lap, 'I am not often so silly; but——' She could say no more.

'You are tired; you have danced too much. Why will you persist in thinking yourself so strong?' returned Dr. Lyall impatiently. 'When one is low it is impossible to take cheerful views of things. You have been neglecting yourself as usual; perhaps you have taken no supper? I will fetch you a little wine and water, and a biscuit.'

Dr. Lyall's quiet, matter-of-fact tones roused

Gerda. She had a vexed consciousness that he thought her missish, perhaps hysterical; she could not tell him that real trouble had overtaken her, and made her wretched; she could not sufficiently control her voice to prove this to him; she was obliged to let him fetch the wine and water, and as his will was stronger than hers, she was forced to drink it; but he saw with concern, that, after all, the discomfort was more mental than bodily.

'I wish I could do something for you,' he said in a kind voice, as he set down the emptied glass. Then he saw a sudden expression of gratitude in her swollen eyes.

'You have helped me; you do not know how much you have helped me,' she replied in so low a voice that he had to stoop to catch her meaning.

'I!' he returned in surprise. 'You must make a mistake, Miss Meredith.'

'No, indeed!' and her voice became stronger. 'Do you remember what you said to me yesterday on the Chilverton Road? The words have been ringing in my ears ever since. "We must do the right thing, even if it give us pain." Well, I have been putting those words into practice, and it has given me pain—that is all; but I thank you all the same, Dr. Lyall—I do indeed!'

He was listening intently, and at one point in her sentence a quick flash of joy came into his eyes, but it faded instantly.

'I must not pretend to understand you,' he said gravely; but her meaning was as plain to him as the traces of the tears on her face. 'I was not aware of saying those words to you, but, all the same, I must not disclaim them; they are true, as heaven above us is true,' with sudden energy.

'Yes, I know that now; they came to me like a light in the darkness. That is why I thanked you for saying them.'

'I am glad if they have helped you,' he returned very seriously; 'but I think,' after a moment's hesitation, 'that you would never go far wrong. You have a more tender conscience than most people, and a truer sense of honour.' The words seemed wrung from him, somehow; he was a man who seldom paid compliments, and even in her despondency Gerda felt a thrill of pride as she heard them. 'Now I must bid you good-bye, for everyone will be leaving. I shall not see you again, but——'

'What will your sister think of me?' she interrupted. 'I must go to her.'

'Indeed, you must do nothing of the kind,' was the reply. 'I will give her a message —a dozen if you like—but you are only fit to go to your own room.' And Gerda felt the wisdom of this advice.

'Very well. Will you give her my love, and ask her to come to-morrow? Then I shall not see you again, Dr. Lyall?'

'I think not—no, I am certain you will not,' forming the instant resolution to keep away from the perilous atmosphere of Chesterton Hall.

Gerda had risen as she spoke, and stood looking very slim and young in her white gown.

'So it is good-bye, you see,' he went on quickly, as he took her hand. 'Take care of yourself, Miss Meredith.' This was all he could find to say, but for many a night he remembered the girl as she stood there before him, with that careworn, weary look on her face. If he had known how soon they were to meet, he would not have gone away with that sudden weight on his mind. As it was, he only called himself a fool, and addressed a few crushing remarks to Pamela, when, with her usual want of tact, she questioned him about his gravity. She punished him, however, by receiving Gerda's message very coolly.

'Mrs. Meredith and Doris both asked me,' she replied curtly. 'I have promised to go to luncheon, and Gertrude is to come too. They want us to help entertain the gentlemen; they do not leave before the afternoon train. And Doris says there are too many for her and her sister to manage.'

'It is a good thing you are going to take Pamela home, Dr. Lyall,' observed Mrs. Hake mischievously. 'I think that poor Mr. Vincent ought to have a hint given him. I am not quite sure he would have approved of that flirtation with Mr. Seymour. In my time an engaged girl never danced more than twice with the same gentleman.'

'As you are both so disagreeable, I shall go to bed,' returned Pamela, with dignity. 'Alick is as cross as two sticks—not that that is anything new, only he is generally better-tempered before people — and as for you,

Gertrude, matrimony has not improved you. —I am sorry to speak so plainly, Captain Hake, but you ought to keep your wife in better order.'

And, with this parting fling, Pamela withdrew to sit by her fire in her smart dressing-gown, and read over Derrick Vincent's last letter for the fifth time ; and as she laid it down there was a pucker on her forehead.

' If Derrick were not so Derrick-like !' she muttered. ' I begin to despair of him. He will never alter—no more shall I. Oh, why —why did I ever care for him if he is always going to make me miserable ?' and Pamela's eyebrows nearly met her hair as she sat there staring into the fire, until she looked like a little old witch in her striped scarlet and black peignoir.

' She has refused him,' was Dr. Lyall's last waking thought before he fell asleep in the dark wintry morning. ' It is strange ! But, then, women do act strangely — one can never predicate their actions with certainty. I should have said any girl would be safe and happy with Hamlyn. But there, it is no concern of mine. Why should I pretend to be glad ? As though her refusing another man had anything to do with me! I vow it will be a long time before I take a week's holiday again, unless I go abroad. Pamela shall not wheedle me to Braeside again in a hurry;' and as Dr. Lyall registered this mental vow he turned over and fell asleep.

Gerda had slipped away to her room, and Doris was the bearer of her excuses: 'Gerda had a headache, and was too tired to come down. She wished them all good-night.' But Doris faltered over her little speech, and looked very guilty as she caught Gerard's eye.

'Oh, Gerda! how could you go and do it?' she had began reproachfully when she found her sister alone, but Gerda cut her short.

'Doris, I cannot talk to you to-night; you must say nothing to me—not one word!' and then she had given her message and closed her door, disregarding Doris's piteous look. But her heart smote her, and she opened it again. 'Kiss me, Dorrie dear, and say good-night. And don't look so miserable; it will not help me, or him either;' and her lip quivered as she turned away.

Gerda knew that she would have a difficult part to play the next day, and would need all her strength to play it well. Gerard would not tell his uncle of the failure of his hopes until their guests had left the Hall, and it would tax all their ingenuity to act so naturally that Sir Godfrey's sharp old eyes should detect nothing wrong. Sir Godfrey had indeed put a question, when the young men had betaken themselves to the smoking-room, and Gerard had lingered behind them for a moment.

'I suppose you have nothing to tell me that would interest me, eh, Gerard?' with a keen look at his nephew.

'No, sir; I believe not,' was the quiet reply, and Sir Godfrey looked disappointed. Nevertheless, he went off to bed, happily quite unconscious that Gerard had played his last card.

'In my time a young fellow would not have shilly-shallied as Gerard is doing,' he grumbled, as he took the loose silver out of his pocket and regarded it admiringly—it was his winnings, the money he had duly and lawfully earned by his own skilful play. '"Strike while the iron is hot!" is my motto. "Blow cold, blow hot," never answered in love matters. Young men are too lazy to make love properly nowadays; they think they have only got to beckon to a girl, and she will come to their call like a tame greyhound.'

Gerard would willingly have gone to bed, too; he felt fagged in body and mind. But his guests held a different opinion.

'We must have a pipe and a palaver, old fellow!' remonstrated Charlie Seymour, and Gerard had to take his part in the lively discussion that followed.

Breakfast was not until a late hour the next morning, and Gerda, who always poured out the tea and coffee, found the large silver urn a very sufficient screen. Charlie Seymour, who was the first to arrive on the scene, thought both the young ladies were unaccountably grave. Doris, who shared her sister's depression, was quite monosyllabic in her replies.

'I expect their mother has given them a wigging,' thought the astute youth after a stolen glance at Gerda's lowered eyelids and Doris's frightened blue eyes. 'Never trust a soft-spoken woman who seems as though butter would not melt in her mouth. She is pretty sure to be a termagant in private.'

But, happily oblivious of this criticism, Mrs. Meredith at this moment smiled so sweetly at him that Charlie grew red and stammered some sort of reply.

'Doris and I are so tired. I wish you would talk for us,' whispered Gerda; and Charlie nodded a cheerful assent.

For the rest of breakfast-time his lively flow of nonsense never ceased; and when the meal was over, he challenged the gentlemen to another tennis-match, leaving the girls to huddle over the fire in their easy-chairs, with their work and books, while Mrs. Meredith and the servants tried to bring order out of the chaotic ball-room of last night.

Doris tried vainly to make Gerda talk, but the latter obstinately refused to open her lips; so Doris at last went off in despair to her mother's help, until Mrs. Hake and Pamela arrived—looking blooming from a long walk in the cold air, and both ready for a long, delicious gossip.

Things went more comfortably after this. Pamela and Charlie Seymour renewed their flirtation of the previous evening, and during luncheon Charlie was seen to take his dandy pocket-book out and write an address:

'"Roadside, Cromehurst." Thanks awfully, Miss Lyall. I will be sure to look your brother up when I am in town. My people live in Yorkshire, you know, but now and then my father takes a house for the season when the mater and the girls bully him into it. I am rather a wandering satellite myself —here, there, and everywhere, as the immortal Miss Mowcher remarks. Well, well, man wants but little here below, but wants that little hot, as one of our fellows said when the butler offered him cold buttered toast; for it stands to reason, Miss Lyall, that if you are you, and I I, as Kant tries to prove——' and so on, much to the delight and mystification of Pamela, who dearly loved a joke.

Pamela, who was always candid, and never tried to disguise her real sentiments, averred an open and decided preference for the society of the stronger sex. 'I never met more than half a dozen women in the whole course of my existence,' she was once heard to remark, 'who really interested me, and to whom I could talk for more than half an hour without a mental yawn. Women are either too frivolous or too serious,' continued the young philosopher. 'There is no happy medium. It is either dress, servants or the kingdom of heaven.' For Pamela was not orthodox, and would at times startle her hearers with daring paradoxes or trite sayings, which wholly lacked reverence; but then, as Pamela was the first to allow, she had no bump of reverence.

Pamela had really no time to bestow on Gerda until the fascinating Charlie and the rest of the gentlemen had taken their leave, and then she accosted her with her usual abruptness.

'What is the matter, Miss Meredith? You look utterly fagged, as though you had been dancing for three nights in succession. Why, Gertrude and I are as fresh as possible! I believe I can do with less sleep than most people;' and she looked inquisitively, but not unkindly, at Gerda as she spoke.

'You forget how unused we are to gaiety,' replied Gerda, colouring a little under this scrutiny. 'Doris and I feel quite dissipated. Are you going by the early train to-morrow?'

'I suppose so. Alick has turned restless —I may say fidgety—and even grudges me time for packing. It is no use my telling him that I dislike to hurry myself. When my lord is in this mood, argument only makes him worse. By-the-bye, he desires his kind regards—let me see: " Please to remember me very kindly to Mrs. Meredith, and to every member of the family "—yes, I think those were his very words.'

'Please remember us to him,' returned Gerda hurriedly.

'Very well, if I do not forget. Dear me! Gertrude is wrapping herself up in her furs. Don't you love sable, Miss Meredith? I think I share the love of a pussy-cat for soft, warm things. If I had that mantle I should always be stroking myself and purring with enjoyment. Well, good-bye; I see we have to go. I would much rather stay and talk to you; but *au revoir!*' and, in spite of her flippant talk, there was real womanliness and hearty good-will in the kiss she gave Gerda.

As Gerda turned away from the door, she saw Gerard close behind her. He had not approached her the whole of the day, though there had been nothing pointed in his avoidance of her; but now she saw that he had something to say to her.

'They are all off now,' he began hurriedly,

as she waited for a moment, 'and I am thankful to get rid of them. They are capital fellows, all of them; but, really, Seymour gets worse and worse. The way he has carried on all day is enough to make one's head ache. I believe Uncle Godfrey was quite shocked once or twice.'

'He is very nice and very kind-hearted, and no one minds his fun.'

'Miss Lyall did not, certainly;' and then Gerard stopped and cleared his throat, and then began again: 'Look here, Gerda, I want to say something; it is no use putting it off. Uncle Godfrey is bound to know, and we may as well get it over. One day is as good as another when one has anything disagreeable to do;' and Gerard gave an uneasy laugh.

'You may tell him whenever you like, Gerard. You are quite right; procrastination never helped anyone yet.'

'Thanks; I thought you would agree with me. Uncle Godfrey will put himself and everyone else in a fuss—he always does, you know—but you need not mind it; and, Gerda, while we are about it, I may just as well say one thing more—if it will make you more comfortable, I will go away for a bit; I'll run up to town and have a look round, and perhaps Seymour will ask me down to Airdale.'

'There is no need for you to go away,' returned Gerda, in a distressed tone; but he would not let her finish.

'It will make things easier for us both, and when I come back we will try and forget all about this;' and Gerard nodded to her with his old kind smile, and turned on his heel and went straight to the library, where Sir Godfrey was dozing over his book.

Gerda caught her breath with a little sob as she looked after him, and asked herself, for the twentieth time, why a girl's heart should be made so hard, and why she could not love this simple, loyal gentleman, with his true English nature—at once so honest and so brave. And Doris, sitting by the fireside, was thinking much the same thing.

'No one but Gerda would have done it,' she sighed.

Gerda stood for a few moments in silent debate with herself; then she joined her mother and sister.

'Mother,' she said impulsively, 'I have

something to tell you that will give you pain. —No, Dorrie, you need not go away'—as Doris rose, and then re-seated herself on a stool at her sister's feet. 'Last night you thought me unkind, but I was too unhappy to talk.—Mother, it is all over between me and Gerard. He has spoken to me again, and it is for the last time.'

'You have refused him? Oh, Gerda, Gerda!' and Mrs. Meredith sank back in her chair, and all her strength left her. What was the use of bringing daughters into the world if they were to inflict such bitter disappointment as this?

'I suppose so; there was nothing else to do. I could not wrong either him or myself. If I had accepted him, it would have been a grievous sin against truth. Oh, it was quite simple,' went on Gerda in a rapt, monotonous tone, as though the fireside circle had an unseen hearer, to whom she was addressing herself; 'it was plain as daylight; one could make no mistake. There can only be one right and one wrong,' she finished, repeating almost unconsciously the doctor's words.

'I don't know what you mean, Gerda,' returned her mother angrily, for she thought her daughter was singularly perverse. 'You were always as fond of Gerard as possible. I remember your grandfather used to call you Gerard's little wife when you were a mere child, and now, just for a girlish whim or fancy, you have thrown him over, and upset the peace of the household.' And Mrs. Meredith looked so flushed and perturbed as she spoke that Charlie Seymour would hardly have thought himself wrong in his uncharitable criticism.

Doris gave her sister's hand a loving little squeeze. She was sorely divided in her sympathies. Her heart was aching for Gerard's disappointment, and last night she had been inclined to be hard on Gerda. But the distress on Gerda's face softened her.

'You could not help it, could you, dear?' she whispered.

'I think Gerda could have helped it if she had taken a little longer time for decision,' observed Mrs. Meredith with illogical severity, for of all women she was the last to advocate matrimony without love. But what is the use of being a woman if one is forced to study logic? 'When so much depends on it, when the peace of an entire household is at stake, there should certainly be more time given for consideration. There was no need to give Gerard a decided answer.'

'Dear mother,' returned Gerda with praiseworthy gentleness, 'would that be treating Gerard well—does he not deserve everything that I can give him? Would it add to his peace of mind or better ensure his ultimate recovery if I had left him in suspense for weeks?'

'It would have given him a chance of winning you.'

'No, mother, no; you are wrong, and Gerard would not agree with you. Neither weeks nor months would make any difference: as soon as I was sure of my own mind, I was right to give him his answer. Mother dear, it is no use talking about it. It is a grievous pity, but it cannot be helped. Doris knows I have tried my best for Gerard.'

'Oh, if Doris was in your confidence——' began Mrs. Meredith rather stiffly.

'Doris was in Gerard's confidence, were you not, Dorrie?' for she had long suspected this; and Doris hung her head and blushed. 'Mother, you are looking at this from Grand's point of view—you are not talking like your dear self at all;' and at this touching appeal Mrs. Meredith's motherly soul seemed to melt within her.

'I am so unhappy, Gerda, but, after all, it is not your fault, you poor child!' and here there was the full kiss of reconciliation with which women always seal their compacts. 'Affection is not to be forced, but it will be very uncomfortable for us all.'

'Gerard wants to go away,' observed Gerda in a low voice; 'he says it will make things easier. But, mother'—as Doris's face grew very long at this—'I would rather go away myself. Grand will not be nice to me for a long time; he will treat me as though I have committed some heinous crime that must shut me out of his favour. Gerard's going away will not help to make home pleasanter to me, but if I take refuge with Aunt Clare the storm will soon blow over.'

'But we shall lose you, Gerda,' returned her mother sorrowfully, for she never liked to part with her girls; they were the only consolations of the widow's heart. In their youth and brightness she found her best happiness. There were times when she hardly knew which she loved best. She was more sure of Doris's sympathy, which was, indeed, never failing; but she relied more on Gerda's strength.

'It will not be for long,' replied Gerda in a coaxing voice, for she was bent on having her way.

Aunt Clare was a friend for adversity, she knew. She had one of those strong, helpful natures which are so restful to weaker folk, and she was never too busy to listen to other people's troubles.

'You must tell Grand that you would like me to go to Aunt Clare for a little,' continued Gerda decidedly; and then Mrs. Meredith sighed, and promised that she would do her best.

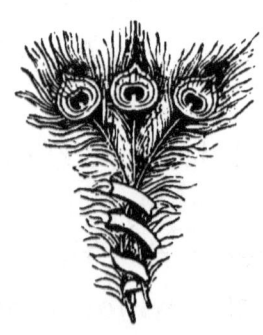

CHAPTER XIII.

SIR GODFREY HAS A TOUCH OF GOUT.

' If you are going to visit the wolf, take your dogs with you.'—*Proverb of Montenegro.*

' In growing old we become more foolish—and more wise.'
—LA ROCHEFOUCAULD.

WHILE Gerda was discussing her future plans somewhat soberly with her mother and sister, Gerard was having rather a bad time with Sir Godfrey.

A threatened touch of gout, which had just heralded its approach by a premonitory twinge or two, had by no means sweetened Sir Godfrey's temper, and on Gerard's broad shoulders fell the first shock of the old man's bitter disappointment.

Gerard bore it for some minutes with his usual passive good-nature, only shrugging his shoulders when a more angry invective or hard cutting speech reached his ears, but he presently entered his protest.

'After all, Uncle Godfrey,' he remarked coolly, 'the disappointment is more mine than yours. There is not the slightest need for all this vituperation. If you excite yourself in this unseemly manner, you will only bring on an attack of gout. All the talk in the world will not mend matters. Gerda has a right to say whom she will or will not marry, and it is no blame to her if she cannot make up her mind to take me. I shall certainly not give her the chance of refusing me again,' for this was the line of action that Sir Godfrey was pressing on his grand-nephew. 'I am not quite such an ass as that. I have done all I can to carry out your wishes and my own too, and it is no fault of mine that I have failed.'

'I am not blaming you,' retorted Sir Godfrey angrily, for this manly expostulation was not without effect on him. 'I am only disgusted that any girl should have had the bad taste to refuse you. It is just Gerda's obstinacy; she has always been obstinate from a child; her mother has spoilt her; she has given way to her in everything, and this is the result.'

'I cannot say that I agree with you,' replied Gerard; 'you are a little bit down just now, but by-and-by, when you think over things quietly, you will take a different view of it all. Look here, Uncle Godfrey, I must just say one thing—I hope you do not mean to speak to Gerda about this; it will do no good, and only increase the general discomfort. I think I have the right to ask this.'

'You may tell the girl that I wash my hands of her and the whole business from this day forth,' returned Sir Godfrey irritably; 'she is an ungrateful child, and I shall take no farther trouble with her. My little Dorrie is worth two of her. Mark my words, Gerard, one day she will repent of this foolish conduct, and then my young lady will be trying to lure you back. Could you not make love to someone else, just in pretence, you know? There is nothing a woman will not do to oust a rival.'

But as Gerard refused somewhat shortly to do any such thing, Sir Godfrey lapsed into fretful sullenness.

'I told you so, mother,' observed Gerda wearily, as they stood by the drawing-room fire. They had just risen from the dinner-table, but Doris and Gerard had not followed them. 'I am to be sent to Coventry. Grand will not speak to me or look at me. Of course, Rogers and Dalton know that I am in disgrace. Dalton was so sorry for me that he handed me the vanilla cream twice. There was something quite persuasive in his manner as he brought it the second time, and when I refused it he looked quite sorrowful.'

'If all our meals are to be like this,' sighed Mrs. Meredith, 'I think I shall plead indisposition, and absent myself from the table. Every mouthful that I took seemed to choke me. Your grandfather is angry with me as well as with you. When anything goes wrong, it is always I who have to bear the blame. He will open his mouth to neither of us—I can see that plainly.'

'Poor dear mother! and it is all my fault;' and Gerda kissed her remorsefully. 'I wish I were a good girl like Doris. Doris will never make anyone's heart ache; but never mind, Grand will not long be vexed with you —you are too necessary to his comfort; he cannot do without you. If he will not speak to me, I must just speak to him, that is all;' and the very next day Gerda carried out her intention. Gerda had never been afraid of her grandfather: her keen young eyes had long ago taken his true measure—his dignity, his arbitrary will and hot temper—and his small, narrow views of life were regarded by her with pitying toleration. In her independent, girlish fashion she had been good to him; but she had never comported herself towards him with Doris's meek submission. If Sir Godfrey had ordered Doris to marry her cousin she would have opened her blue eyes with intense amazement, and would have accepted him without a moment's hesitation; but, then, Doris had no indefinite yearnings after an ideal, and in an unconscious, simple way she already loved Gerard, though neither she nor he guessed that fact. Doris was one of those happy-minded people who can suit themselves to any environment; one could predict safely that she would make a cheerful old maid or a proud wife and mother, whichever condition Providence might allot to her. And yet, in her own sweet maidenly way, Doris had her aspirations.

'It must be so nice to be very, very fond

of someone,' she had once said to Gerda; but even this modest hint cost Doris many blushes.

Sir Godfrey looked up with cold surprise when Gerda entered the library. It was not possible for him to be more erect—his stiff old back was always rigidly upright; but there was something majestic and judicial in the way he laid down his book and regarded his grand-daughter, and there was withering sarcasm in the tone in which he said:

'I was not aware that I sent for you, Gerda.'

But Gerda was equal to the occasion, and there was no temper in her voice as she answered:

'No, grandfather, and I am afraid that you do not want to see me; but there is something that I must say to you.'

'Indeed!' and, after drawling out this word, Sir Godfrey took up his book again.

Under such circumstances her mother and Doris would have retired humbly; but Gerda had too much spirit to submit to injustice; she intended Sir Godfrey to listen to her, and if he wished to be uncivil and keep his eyes on his book, he could not protect his ears without absolute rudeness, so she went on without hesitation :

'Of course I see you are angry with me, Grand—anyone could see that, when you take so little trouble to hide it; but there is no need for you to be angry with mother, too : she wanted me to marry Gerard quite as much as you did, only, being a woman, she is a little more reasonable about it. In these sort of cases women understand each other best.'

Sir Godfrey settled his pince-nez more firmly on his nose, and glared at his granddaughter. His finely-formed old hand trembled slightly during the process.

'Did you intrude yourself into my presence to talk about your mother?' he asked, in a cutting tone. 'With regard to yourself, I have nothing to say—nothing at all; and I beg,' somewhat hastily, 'that you will not seat yourself. When I was young, children used to stand until their parents desired them to sit down. Ah, you may smile,' as Gerda's lip curled a little. 'I am quite aware that obedience to parents, and reverence, and courtesy, have gone out of fashion—out of fashion.'

'There is no need for me to sit down. I never mind standing,' replied Gerda quietly—and, indeed, her slim young figure seemed to require no support. 'I am glad we did not live in those dark ages, Grand. Children could hardly have loved their parents in those days, if they did not venture to sit in their presence—and I think love is better than anything.'

'Oh, you think so, do you? Have you anything further to remark?'

'Yes, dear, a great deal more,' she returned cheerfully. 'I want to tell you how sorry I am to disappoint you and mother—as to poor Gerard, I am more than sorry for him—but it cannot be helped. One must be true to one's conscience before everything. I cannot love Gerard well enough to marry him, and I was obliged to tell him so. The whole thing is between him and me—no one has any right to meddle with it, or to be angry.'

But this clear and sensible statement did not commend itself to Sir Godfrey, and a sudden twinge of gout and conscience together lent anger to his tone.

'I have every right to be angry,' he returned, bringing down his hand sharply on the table. 'Who has a better right, I should like to know? Have I not fed and clothed you from your babyhood? Is it not my roof that shelters you and your mother and sister? Is it not my bread you eat? And what return do you make me? You thwart me in my dearest wish—just for a girlish whim, or obstinacy, you refuse the finest young fellow in the world; and yet I am not to tell you to your face that you are an ungrateful girl.'

'You may tell me what you like, Grand,' returned Gerda rather sadly. 'I think I mind your hard words less than your silence —silence can be so cruelly hard; but, all the same, there seems little use in speaking such words. When two people look at the same thing from different points of view there can be no agreement. You choose to think,' she went on, after a moment, 'that I have refused Gerard out of mere perversity. How am I to persuade you to the contrary? I might talk for an hour, and you would not understand me! I think,' folding her hands together, and looking down with a graceful patience in her attitude, 'that it would be wiser and better to keep my thoughts to myself.'

'I think so, too, and that we may as well close this interview. I have nothing else to say to you, Gerda. You have disappointed me, and you cannot be surprised if I lose interest in you.'

'No,' in a slow, pondering voice. 'I ought not to be surprised when I remember Aunt Clare.' And as an uneasy flush came to Sir Godfrey's brow at the mention of his daughter's name, she continued quickly: 'There is one thing I must speak to you about—that I think you ought to hear—and that is, that Gerard talks of going away.'

'In other words, you are driving him from his home.'

'If you put it in that way, I suppose I must say "yes." But I think it is for me to go—not for him.'

'I think so, too!' and Sir Godfrey evidently meant what he said, for he hated to part with Gerard.

'May I go to Aunt Clare, then? It will be far, far better for you and Gerard, and every-one, if I go away. Mother will fret herself ill with worry; and Doris will be as miserable as possible. And I tell you frankly, Grand, that if you cannot bring yourself to forgive me, I would rather not stay at home. It is not pleasant to see the servants finding out one's little secrets—and if you will not speak to me at meal-times, of course they will know all about it.'

Sir Godfrey put up his hand to silence her.

'I have had enough of this chattering,' he said curtly. 'You may go where you like, and stay away as long as you like. This is the last word I mean to say on the subject. When Gerard comes in from the farm you may send him to me;' and this time Sir Godfrey took up his book with a determined air, and turned his back on his grand-daughter.

Gerda quietly withdrew. She had said all she wanted to say, and had obtained her end—permission to go to her aunt Clare; the interview, unpleasant as it had been, had not depressed her. Her grandfather had said hard things to her, but she had expected him to say them; she must give him time to get over his disappointment; when she had gone away they would all settle down comfortably, and in time he would forgive her.

When she gave the message to Gerard,

half an hour later, he looked at her searchingly.

'You ought not to have gone near him,' he said reproachfully. 'You must leave me to fight your battles.'

'There was something that I was obliged to ask him,' she replied apologetically. 'Thank you, Gerard, for what you have done for me. Grand is terribly angry; but I dare say it will only be for a time.'

'All the same, you ought to have left him to me;' and then Gerard went off to the library. But a little later he came out with a perturbed face, and went in search of his cousin. Her found her in the morning-room sorting some music.

'Gerda,' he said abruptly, 'I want you to tell me the truth. Is it your own wish to go to Cromehurst, or is Uncle Godfrey sending you away for the purpose of keeping me here? It is impossible to find out anything, when he rambles on in that roundabout fashion. He was so incoherent that I told him at last that I should come and ask you the question. Gerda, you know there is no need for this at all. I told you yesterday that I should go away.'

'But if I really want to go?' she pleaded. 'Gerard, you don't know how I long for Aunt Clare. I am so fond of her. She is like a dear elder sister more than an aunt; and she is such a comfortable person when one is in any little trouble or difficulty. Grand made no objection when I asked him: "You may go where you like, and stay away as long as you like." Surely no permission could be more gracious;' but Gerda's joke was a little forced.

'He has got the gout coming on, and it does not improve his temper. I should advise you not to interpret his speeches too literally; he will come round before long. If it be really your own wish to go to Aunt Clare, of course I will not prevent you;' and as Gerda looked at him gratefully, he went back to his uncle.

If Gerda wished to go she should go, and he would never let her know that it was irksome for him to stay at home. To be sure, he had his duties, and perhaps nursing his uncle through an attack of gout might be one of them; but, all the same, he would rather have run up to town and seen a little life with some of his chums. It would be rather deadly staying on at the Hall with Gerda away and Sir Godfrey in a bad temper; but he would remain at his post, for all that, and by-and-by he would get his fling.

Gerda did not let the grass grow under her feet. She wrote that very night to her aunt, and two days afterwards she received the warmest invitation.

'You will be as welcome as flowers in May, darling,' wrote Mrs. Glyn. 'Your uncle Horace looked quite pleased when I gave him your message. "Let her come as soon as she likes, and stop as long as possible." Those were his very words. Want of hospitality was never one of my good husband's faults.'

Mrs. Meredith had a quiet little cry over this letter.

'Clare is my only sister,' she observed plaintively. 'It is very hard that we so seldom meet. When we were girls, we were everything to each other. If only she had not married your uncle Horace!'

'I think she was quite right to marry him,' returned Gerda, with youthful brusquerie, for she always defended her aunt. 'It is not very nice for her to come here without her husband. And then Grand is not kind to her—he always finds fault with everything she says, and puts her down unmercifully. Why do you not go to Cromehurst, mother? She would love to have you.'

'Yes, Clare is a good creature,' replied Mrs. Meredith, with another sigh, and then she let the subject drop. It was not easy for her to explain to her daughter that the society of her brother-in-law was singularly distasteful to her. Clare was her own sister, and even her faults were dear to her, but there could be no comfort for her under the roof of Horace Glyn.

Gerda began her preparations as soon as she received her aunt's letter; and one evening, about a week after the dance, she put the finishing touches to a tea-cloth that she was embroidering for Mrs. Glyn, while Doris sat on the other side of the fireplace, watching her with a disconsolate face, while the well-filled trunk stood open beside her.

'I do hate you to go away, Gerda,' she said at last.

Gerda looked up quickly.

'I don't think you will be dull, Dorrie. Gerard will give you plenty of his company.

Remember, you have promised to take Waif out every day; and then there are the birds and the ferns. I shall write to you very often, and you must tell me all about mother and Gerard.'

But Doris was not to be comforted so easily. She was in a lugubrious mood, and there were uneasy thoughts at work in her girlish head.

'I don't suppose Gerard will be good company,' she returned. 'He will be missing you every moment of the day. If I could only be a little more like you, Gerda! but I am such a stupid little thing, and I am sure Gerard thinks so.'

'I am sure he thinks nothing of the kind;' and Gerda laid down her work and regarded Doris's troubled face with admiring kindness.

'It seems such a pity that one cannot share one's good qualities with other people,' sighed Doris. 'If one could only grow up to—to the person one wants to please; but I could never talk as you do, Gerda; you go so dreadfully deep into things—too deep even for Gerard; but all the same he likes to listen to you. Gerard does not talk much, but he thinks a great deal.'

'How on earth did you find that out, Dorrie?' and Gerda's tone expressed extreme surprise. 'I don't believe Gerard thinks as much as—as other men.'

'You are mistaken there,' returned Doris, with a knowing nod of her head. 'You do not take the trouble to understand Gerard. He has his ideas about everything, and when he talks to me I always feel as though I should never reach his level; somehow,' continued Doris, with a painful effort to explain some truth that she dimly realized, 'you are not fair on Gerard. You make up your mind that he does not care for certain things, and he never takes the trouble to undeceive you. Gerard thinks a good deal.'

'I did not know that you were such a philosopher, Dorrie;' but Gerda's tone was dubious. 'I am not so sure that you are not growing up, after all. Do you know what I read once, and I think you are trying to express much the same thought?—"You cannot teach people to speak your language unless you can speak theirs." I think Gerard and I talk in different languages.'

'But that may not be Gerard's fault!'

'No, dear; it is far more likely to be

mine. I have not a word to say against Gerard. Perhaps I shall grow wiser as I grow older, and not expect so much of other people. I know you have a horror of my quotations, but let me read you what I have written down in what I call my thought-book. They are the words of the same wise queen whose saying I repeated just now. She says: " In youth, one is a mediæval castle, with hidden nooks, secret chambers, mysterious galleries, trenches and ramparts; one becomes afterwards a modern mansion, rich, morocco-leathered, elegant, stylish, and only open to the select; and ultimately a great hall, open to the whole world—a market, a museum, or a cathedral."'

' I am afraid I do not understand all that,' observed Doris, with a sort of despairing resignation. ' What nice talks you and Aunt Clare will have! You will not have only stupid little me for audience. I suppose Gerard and I are the modern mansions, and you are the mediæval castle, with all sorts of subterranean passages? But in my opinion the museum and the cathedral are far higher and more useful.'

' So they are, and you are not so stupid as

you make yourself out to be. Come, cheer up, Dorrie! I am leaving you a grand mission—to take care of mother and Gerard. There, I have finished the border of the tea-cloth. Will not Aunt Clare think it lovely? and Uncle Horace will rebuke us both. He will tell me that I should have been better employed in visiting the poor and teaching the orphans, and he will rail against Aunt Clare for her love of finery. Now will you help me shut my trunk, and then, as it is late, we had better go to bed.'

Gerda was to start early the following morning, and Gerard and Doris were to accompany her to the station. Just before the carriage came round she went into the library to bid Sir Godfrey good-bye. He received her rather coldly, and her kiss met with slight response.

'I suppose you will send your love to Aunt Clare, Grand?' she asked as she stood by him a moment. She quite understood that she was not yet forgiven, and expected no special softness from him; but he was old and ailing, and she could make allowances for him.

'Oh yes, you may give her my love. I

suppose she will come and see us some time this summer, if she can tear herself away from her husband? She may bring one or two of the children with her if she wishes to do so; but your mother will settle all that. There, I hear the carriage. I must beg that you do not keep the horses waiting a moment—not one moment;' but Gerda still lingered.

'Won't you say something kind to me before I go, Grand? Are you still so very angry with me?'

'You have disappointed me,' was his sole reply; but he did not add that it was not in his nature to brook such disappointment.

Gerda looked at him for a moment; then she smoothed back the gray hair from the high, narrow forehead, and kissed him gently between his eyes.

'Good-bye, dear, you will not always be hard on me,' she answered; 'at least, I hope not;' and then she went in quest of her mother.

She was rather silent during the drive, and Gerard talked more to Doris than to her. But as he settled her in the train, and arranged her rug for her, he said in a low voice :

'You will not stay very long away, Gerda ?'

'I do not know; I have not thought about it,' she answered; but as she spoke a curious feeling crept over her—a sudden sense of distance and separation; a strange foreboding that she had reached some turning in her life. She was going away from them, but when and how would she return? The question seemed to oppress her. 'I have not thought about it,' she faltered. 'Goodbye, Gerard; take care of them all for me.' The train moved as she spoke, and he nodded and stepped back on the platform.

Gerda looked at them both rather wistfully—at Gerard's strong, well-built figure and grave face, and then at Doris, as she stood closely beside him. The faint wintry sunshine seemed to envelop them in its transient brightness as they stood together.

'Why should it not be?' she said to herself—'if he only knew, Doris would make him very happy; but,' with a sigh, 'I suppose he will never find that out for himself.'

CHAPTER XIV.

ST. JUDE'S VICARAGE.

'We live with other men, and to other men; neither with nor to ourselves.'—CLARENDON.

'The wavering mind is a base property.'—EURIPIDES.

THE parish of St. Jude's, Cromehurst, where the Rev. Horace Glyn had a cure of souls, was not in the town itself, but in the outlying suburb that had sprung up in mushroom fashion during the last few years, and of which the cemetery was the nucleus and centre.

It was a somewhat straggling parish, and embraced all sorts and conditions of men.

The new roads that branched off from the church in all directions, with their substantial, comfortable houses, were inhabited by respectable business men, who went up to town by the fast early trains, and returned to the bosom of their family in the evening; but on the other side of the cemetery was a poorer neighbourhood, where a motley class, ranging from small shopkeepers and artisans to gutter merchants and flower-girls, took up their abode. At first sight it would appear to the casual observer that the people living in those roomy cottages, with their little plots of garden ground, must be fairly well-to-do, and that no fell grip of poverty had made itself felt in the roads rejoicing in the euphonious names of Acacia and Elm-tree Roads and Hazelbeech Gardens; but this would be drawing an erroneous conclusion.

The heart of man is deceitful and desperately wicked, and not even plenty of space and elbow-room, abundance of fresh water and fine air, could transform the improvident idler into the industrious workman, or lure the drunkard from the public-house, out of which he reeled night after night to his home. Human nature is the same everywhere, and no paradise is free from the trail of the serpent. Even in Hazelbeech Gardens slatternly mothers sent out their unkempt, pale-faced children to play in the gutters, until the hand of authority swept them off to parish and board schools. Therefore was the soul of the Rev. Horace Glyn vexed within him as he walked down the wide roads, or exchanged greetings with a loiterer or two. 'What could they want more?' he asked himself. There was abundance of work for all; no one had intercepted the sweet current of air that blew freshly on them from the open country; no water could be purer; no parish so prodigal of wise, self-supporting charities. The coal-club, the provident fund, the boot and shoe fund, were all flourishing and well sustained, and yet vice and want skulked behind some of those walls; the unrepentant prodigal still fed on husks, and the seven devils had not yet departed out of the Magdalene.

The church of St. Jude's was in all respects what a church should be, but the Vicarage was felt to be a failure. The funds had been low, and the builder's estimates had been so sadly curtailed that anything like ornamentation had been clearly impossible.

Mrs. Glyn's heart had sunk within her as she looked round the rooms, with their barrack-like spaciousness and general barrenness of detail; and while her husband was descanting delightfully on the airy situation, the capital ventilation, and the cheerful view from the windows, she was wondering how she could ever give them a comfortable, home-like aspect.

'The papers are so ugly, Horace,' she could not help saying at last.

'You will soon get used to them, my dear,' he returned encouragingly; 'and, after all, there is very little ground for complaint: the proportions of the rooms are excellent, and there are plenty of them—we shall not be crowded for want of space.' And Mr. Glyn looked so supremely satisfied that she had not the courage to damp him.

Poor Mrs. Glyn! she had an innate love of the beautiful, and those cheap glaring wall-papers haunted her like a nightmare. If only Horace would have allowed her to change the drawing-room one! she thought, but the mere idea had so shocked him that she had been reduced to a discomfited silence. Mrs. Glyn was a high-spirited woman, and her will was a strong one. But her husband's was far stronger; in any such contest she was compelled to yield. There had been times during their married life when she had pleaded earnestly with him for something that she thought necessary to her own or her children's comfort; but though he would listen to her with patience, and give good heed to all her reasoning, the result had always been the same. When she had finished, he would tell her quietly that the thing was impossible, and that it was wrong of her to wish it—that it was a wife's duty to be guided by her husband, and that she should try on all occasions to think with him.

'I am quite sure no wife was ever more submissive to her husband than I am to you, Horace,' she had said once, when his reproof had been more stinging than usual.

'I have never complained,' was his imperturbable answer. 'On the contrary, I believe I have often praised you, and I am quite sure that on this point you will be guided by me;' and such was the power of the man, and so great was her belief in him, that she had invariably yielded to him, sorrowfully, and with much inward reluctance; but still the victory had been his. Perhaps if she had known how he loved and honoured her for her womanly compliance, she might have gone away more comforted; but he was a man of few words, and outward demonstration was by no means easy to him.

The Vicar of St. Jude's prided himself on belonging to no special party. In the language of the great Apostle, he would be all things to all men; he would wear no distinctive badge; neither High Church, Low Church, nor Broad Church should claim him. 'His creed is the Glynian Creed,' an undergraduate was once heard to say; 'he has a platform of his own, and the name of his party is Horace Glyn.' But this severe criticism only grazed the truth. There was nothing colourless or obscure in Horace Glyn's pastoral teaching. On the contrary, he held strong views on all subjects, and there was marked originality and much depth of thought in those short, concise sermons that were preached Sunday after Sunday at St. Jude's. Perhaps his chief defect lay in his unmitigated contempt for the small aims and narrower views of the puerile souls around him; and he was specially hard on the honest business men who composed part of his congregation. For them he seemed to have no pity or scruple; for their sakes he would utter the most startling paradoxes: for in one breath he would tell them that work was the salt and savour of life, and the next he would reproach them with their love of greed, their absorbing preoccupation with the perishing things of this life; and he was always so terribly in earnest that many a slumbering conscience was roused and pricked into uneasiness.

And there was another thing that added weight to his influence—he was so absolutely true, and he so evidently believed every word he spoke. At times there was something almost pathetic in the way he strove to live up to his conviction, and when he failed to do so he would accuse himself almost bitterly of his want of faithfulness.

With all these virtues, it must still be acknowledged that Horace Glyn was more respected than loved, and he was regarded even by his children with a species of awe; his affection for his wife and children bordered on intensity, and in his own heart he would plead guilty to over-much tenderness, but he seldom allowed them to perceive this. The small every-day jokes, the light, innocent play of nonsense and repartee, that make family life so pleasant, were missing at

St. Jude's Vicarage; the weight of the paternal gravity was too severe a pressure on the youthful spirits; and it was often remarked by visitors how quiet and well-behaved the children were in their father's presence.

'You should see them with me,' Mrs. Glyn would answer. 'I think they keep all their nonsense for my private ear. Horace is so very grave, and then he is often so pre-occupied, and they are afraid of troubling him. They know nothing ever troubles me; I think I am a child still, I am so fond of noise and play.'

It was towards evening when Gerda and her luggage were driven up to the door of St. Jude's Vicarage. She was weary and benumbed with her long, cold journey, but as the door was flung open, before the cabman could descend from his box, and she saw the stream of warm light, and Mrs. Glyn's tall figure, with the neat maid-servant behind her, she forgot her fatigue, and ran eagerly up the steps.

'Oh, Aunt Clare, how nice it is to see you again!'

'You are late, dearest. Bessie and I were

just beginning to get anxious. Oh, how cold you are! Do not stand in this bitter draught another moment. Lydia will look after the luggage;' and so saying, Mrs. Glyn led the way to the bright, comfortable drawing-room.

A girl about sixteen was sitting reading by the fire, with a tabby cat curled up in her lap. She rose at once as the visitor entered the room.

'Why, Bessie, how you have grown!' exclaimed Gerda, kissing her. 'You are quite a young lady now.'

Bessie blushed and looked pleased. She was a fair, pretty-looking girl, with gentle, retiring manners; but she was evidently very shy and unformed. She drew the easy-chair closer to the fire, and looked at her mother as though for further directions.

'Yes, dear, you may go and bring Gerda a cup of hot tea. Make it yourself, Bessie, for Rebecca is busy;' and Bessie at once left the room.

'Bessie is growing very pretty,' observed Gerda; 'but I see she is as quiet as ever. So the children are away, Aunt Clare; I am so sorry not to see them. I shall miss my romps with Janie and Nora; and then there is Willie;' and here she stopped and looked at her aunt a little anxiously.

Mrs. Glyn's face grew grave.

'They are spending the remainder of the holidays with their Aunt Emma—I think I told you so in my letter—and Willie will go straight to school from there. Of course I was sorry about it, but Horace seemed to think it was best; but I see so little of Willie now;' and then Mrs. Glyn sighed and changed the subject by questioning Gerda about her journey.

Gerda could have found it in her heart to echo her aunt's sigh. There was more in these few words than met the ear. Horace Glyn's eldest sister was by no means beloved by her sister-in-law. Mrs. Harding was a bustling, managing woman, with clear, worldly views, and she had some influence with her brother. She had married a man much older than herself, and to make matters worse in Mrs. Glyn's eyes, Mr. Harding had a large retail business, and 'the shop,' as she called it, was a bitter humiliation to her.

It was in vain that her husband represented to her that nothing could be more respectable than Mrs. Harding's position.

Clare only shuddered at the word 'respectability.' To be sure, her sister-in-law had a handsome house at Highgate, and drove in her own carriage; but even this failed to give Mrs. Glyn satisfaction. Mr. Harding might be respectable, but in her eyes he was hopelessly vulgar. He had a loud, joking manner, which always offended her, and even his good-nature and his liberality to her children could elicit no commendation from her lips. And there was another thing that had widened the breach between the sisters-in-law: Mrs. Harding, with her shrewd commonsense, often influenced her brother, and it was owing to her and her husband Willie had had that presentation to Christ's Hospital.

The greatest sorrow of Clare's life had been the loss of her second child—a beautiful boy who had died of croup in his third year; but it may be said that the bitterest humiliation she had ever suffered was when she first saw her youngest born attired in the quaint mediæval dress that has so strangely lingered into the nineteenth century.

But it was in vain that she had striven

with her husband in a hot, tearful argument that had driven him for once to anger.

'Horace, I cannot bear it,' she had said to him. 'This is Emma's doing; she has harped on this ever since Willie was born; but you have no right to listen to her and not think of your wife's feelings. Why do you not teach him yourself if you cannot afford to send him to school?' for as yet the living of St. Jude's had not been offered to him.

'You are talking at random, Clare,' returned her husband coldly, for this false pride, as he called it, made him less patient with her than usual. 'How am I to teach Willie when my time is not my own? Would you have me defraud the sick and dying that Willie may have his Latin lessons? Is this your idea of a curate's duty?'

'I will teach him myself, then—I will, indeed, Horace!' she exclaimed eagerly. 'I know a little Latin even now, and I can learn more. Let me have him for a year or two until we grow a little richer; he is my boy as well as yours, and I have a right to be consulted.'

'But you have no right to lose your

temper,' with a disapproving glance at her flushed face, 'and least of all with your husband.' Then, as she burst into tears, he relented and took her hand. 'My love, this is absolutely wrong and foolish. Why cannot you trust me to do the best I can for Willie? Do you think that I would not much rather send him to Rugby or Harrow? I was a Rugby boy myself. But in our position—with all these children to educate, and on small means—there should be no room for pride. I have done all I can for Walter, but there is nothing to spare for Willie; and when Antony promised to secure me a presentation to Christ's Hospital I dared not refuse it.'

'It is all Emma,' she returned in despair; 'she has more influence with you than I have, Horace. I have seen that for a long time.'

'Is it necessary to wound me with such speeches?' he asked reproachfully. 'How have I ever failed to you, Clare, except by loving you too well?' Then, at the break of tenderness in his voice, she crept closer to him.

'Please forgive me,' she whispered; 'but

I am so unhappy, Horace. If we could only think alike about this; if you would put yourself in my place for once! Think of what my father and Honoria will say! I have so often heard father call it "a charity school for gentlemen."'

'True,' he returned with a curl of his lip, 'and Charles Lamb and Samuel Taylor Coleridge were charity boys. But what of that, Clare? Why should not our Willie follow their footsteps? Has not Christ's Hospital turned out brave gentlemen and learned scholars? My dear, try to be sensible. If Willie's yellow stockings offend your eyes, that is a small grievance weighed in the balance against more solid advantages. You have often blamed Emma, in my hearing, for her worldly motives; but take care that you are free yourself from the same taint. Such pride as yours is only a subtler form of worldliness. Do not let us argue any more upon a foregone conclusion. I have already made up my mind, and the thing must be done.'

But though, as usual, Horace Glyn had his way, in his heart he was very sorry that necessity had obliged him to inflict this humiliation on his wife; as far as his conscience permitted him, he would willingly have pleased her, and his anger had been roused by her inability to perceive this conflict that was for ever going on between his inclination and duty. Not that yellow stockings were so odious to him, for nature had not endowed him with a fine cultured taste—he was a robust Philistine of the old type; nevertheless, he loved his wife dearly, and he hated to see a cloud on her bright face, and to know that he himself had brought it there made him thoroughly unhappy.

Gerda knew all about this trouble. Willie had been at Christ's Hospital for three years now, but his mother still secretly lamented the fact; and though she had long ago forgiven her husband, the breach between her and her sister-in-law had never been healed.

Her husband did not trouble himself to effect a reconciliation. He was wise enough to perceive that the natures of the two women were too dissimilar to render harmony possible. He never pressed his wife to accompany him to Highgate; neither did he insist on her receiving his sister; he left all that to time and chance. But he took care that his children did not fail in their duty to their aunt; and as Mrs. Harding had no children of her own, and was fond of the society of young people, she frequently invited her nephews and nieces to stay with her.

The twins and Willie always enjoyed their visits to The Briars. They liked driving into town with Aunt Emma, and watching her numerous purchases. Then Uncle Harding would take them to the pantomime; or they would go to the Zoological Gardens, or to Madame Tussaud's, or other places of amusement, under the care of a gray old clerk. But these visits were less relished by Walter and Bessie; and Bessie, in particular, grew silent and home-sick under her aunt's wing.

Gerda sipped her hot tea, and basked pleasantly in the warmth while she answered Mrs. Glyn's eager questions.

'You are looking thinner, Aunt Clare,' she said at last.

But Mrs. Glyn only laughed, and disclaimed this. She was a very graceful-looking woman, and many people thought her extremely handsome, though her hair was tinged with gray and there were lines under the frank, smiling eyes, but in her husband's eyes she had never ceased to be lovely.

'Yes, indeed, you are thinner,' repeated Gerda tenderly. 'You work too hard, Aunt Clare. I mean to tell Uncle Horace so when I see him. I am right, am I not, Bessie?' as the girl looked up rather quickly at this.

'Hold your tongue, Bessie,' returned her mother good-humouredly. 'I will not have you two conspiring against my peace. One master is enough for any woman.'

'Mother always works too hard,' observed Bessie in a low voice; 'and she does more than ever now that she teaches Janie and Nora.'

'Oh, Aunt Clare!' in quite a shocked tone of voice.

But Mrs. Glyn only shook her head reproachfully at Bessie.

'Mouse! I am surprised at you,' for this was Bessie's sobriquet in the family. 'Gerda will give me no peace now. No, you shall not speak; I must explain matters. You see, since Miss Hall left us we have not had a governess. Your uncle Horace hates schools for girls; and, really, Walter is likely to cost us so much that we could hardly afford to send them, even though Mrs. Vincent's terms are certainly very moderate, so I suggested that I should teach them myself, and your uncle thought this such a good plan that I have done so ever since Michaelmas—and I assure you that I like the work immensely.'

'Yes, but it is too much for you, with the house and all your parish work; how can Uncle Horace allow you to overtax your strength? You mentioned Mrs. Vincent just now—I seem to have heard that name before.'

'She is Dr. Lyall's sister—such a charming person! Even your uncle Horace can find no fault with her, though he has such a high standard for people. By-the-by, Gerda, you have become quite intimate with Pamela and her brother. You know, they are both great favourites of mine. I shall want to hear all about everything—the ice accident, and the party, and—and other things'—and here she looked meaningly at her niece's averted face—'but we shall have plenty of time for all that to-morrow. Let us go upstairs now, and then you can rest and refresh yourself before dinner ;' and as Gerda approved of this suggestion, Mrs. Glyn led the way upstairs to the room that had been prepared for the guest.

CHAPTER XV.

TWILIGHT CONFIDENCES.

'There will be always cross-lights troubling the earnest soul.'—LORD HOUGHTON.

MRS. GLYN had evidently made up her mind that all awkward topics should be avoided that first evening. Her tired guest was to be warmed, welcomed and refreshed; she was to be petted and made to feel at home. There would be plenty of time for talk presently, when Gerda should have recovered from the fatigue of her journey.

Late dinner was an innovation at St. Jude's Vicarage. Mrs. Glyn, who knew how her husband suffered from the effects of the hurried mid-day meal, had been urgent with him to permit himself this one indulgence; but, as usual, her arguments had not prevailed. She had found an unexpected ally, however, in Dr. Lyall, who had been called in to prescribe for the overworked Vicar.

'Your digestion is seriously impaired,' he had said to him; 'you have been in the habit of snatching a hurried meal in the midst of your parish work.—If you value your husband's health, Mrs. Glyn, let him have a comfortable dinner at seven o'clock; a light luncheon is all that he ought to have at mid-day.'

Mr. Glyn had not openly rebelled against his doctor's wishes, but when he had been left alone with his wife he had looked very solemn.

'It will double our weekly expenses, Clare,' he observed with a grave face; but on this point his wife reassured him.

'I think you are wrong, dear,' she returned gently; 'it will not make all that difference. Let us try for a week or so, by way of experiment;' and this time she was allowed to carry her point. Mrs. Glyn was an excellent manager, and after a few demurs from her husband, that grew fainter and fainter, the late dinner became a permanent institution at the Vicarage.

Mr. Glyn's health had improved under this

régime, but his ascetic soul had secret qualms of conscience, and from time to time he explained laboriously to a chance guest that he was unwillingly carrying out his doctor's prescriptions. 'No man should be a slave to his own appetite,' he would say, as he carved the slices of roast beef. 'I am not indifferent to creature comforts, but I like to feel that I can do without them'—and in all justice it must be owned that no man could so well dispense with luxuries.

When Gerda returned to the drawing-room, she found Mr. Glyn in possession of the hearthrug. He was holding forth to his family on some point that had come under his notice, but as she entered the room he stopped at once and greeted her most cordially. Mr. Glyn was a striking-looking man; he was not tall, but his erect figure and a certain fine carriage of the head gave him an air of unusual dignity. His features were good, and there was a keenness and brightness in his eyes which struck terror into evildoers, and it was difficult indeed for anyone with an uneasy conscience to meet without flinching that clear penetrating gaze.

But at times when things went well with him, and he found himself alone with his wife and children, there would be a softness and sweetness of expression that made up for his want of demonstration; and as he kissed Gerda, and asked her kindly about her journey, it was evident that this mood was on him now.

'Why, Walter, I should hardly have known you!' exclaimed Gerda, as a tall, good-looking young fellow shook hands with her, and she drew her finger significantly across her upper lip.

'You did not know that Walter was cultivating a moustache,' observed his father dryly; but he was secretly proud of his son's hirsute ornament. 'He is afraid of looking two young for an undergraduate—eh, Walter?' But Walter only reddened, and exchanged a quick glance with his mother.

'I suppose your aunt has told you that we hope to send Walter to Oxford next term?' continued Mr. Glyn; but his wife interrupted him.

'No, indeed, Horace. I have told Gerda nothing yet; home politics are not for tired travellers, and Gerda looks extremely fatigued.

Ah, there is the dinner-bell;' and then the conversation was suspended until the Vicar had said grace.

Mr. Glyn was determined to make himself pleasant; he asked after Sir Godfrey and every member of the family with a fine assumption of interest.

'Sir Godfrey wears well, but he must be getting old,' he observed, as though he and Sir Godfrey were the best of friends: 'he is a fine specimen of the old country gentleman.'

'Grandfather was seventy-five last birthday,' returned Gerda; 'he is very proud of the fact, and is always reminding us of it.' Then Mrs. Glyn sighed, and her husband looked at her and proceeded to talk of Gerard.

'He leads rather a useless existence, I am afraid,' he remarked with some severity; 'shooting, and fishing, and cricket, can hardly fill up a man's life.' Then Gerda, with some embarrassment, tried to defend her cousin.

'Gerard is never idle,' she said quietly; 'you have no idea how busy he is from morning to night, and he helps Grand so much too : he keeps his accounts for him, and does a good deal of his business. Grand does not really think himself old, but he gets dreadfully muddled sometimes ; and then Gerard makes everything straight for him.'

'I suppose Hamlyn will be getting a wife soon,' observed Mr. Glyn, for he was ignorant of the family scheme. Then Gerda blushed violently and held her peace, while Mrs. Glyn came to her rescue.

'I suppose it will be his duty to marry some day,' she said in a matter-of-fact tone ; 'but there is plenty of time for that. Gerda, I wish you would tell us a little about your accident. Dr. Lyall refused to say a word when he was here on Tuesday ; by-the-by, I told him that you were coming, and he said his sister would be so pleased. I am glad you like Pamela—is she not an amusing little person ?—only I regret to say your uncle does not admire her.'

'I am sorry to hear that, Uncle Horace. I have taken such a fancy to Miss Lyall ; she is so thoroughly original, and says such clever things.'

Then Mr. Glyn gave an eloquent dissenting shrug which seemed to amuse his wife.

'Ask him why he does not like her, Gerda!' But Mr. Glyn did not wait to be questioned.

'In the first place I deny her originality. It is quite true that she does not talk in the usual conventional way—she has evidently cultivated the art of saying odd, out-of-the-way things; she wishes to appear clever, but in reality she is flighty.'

'I do not agree with you, Uncle Horace.'

'Neither do I, Gerda; he is dreadfully hard on Pamela: there is never any peace when he is in the room with her; somehow she rubs him up the wrong way.'

'She should talk more sensibly,' he returned severely. 'What do you think she said the other day, Gerda? I was talking about her sister—ah, poor thing! I forgot that you do not know her; but she is a most pleasing person. I was saying something civil about her, and Miss Lyall suddenly began abusing her: she did not know why I always praised her sister, I was not generally so easily satisfied with people. Hester was well enough, but she was a very ordinary person; her conscientiousness amounted to a fault—she hated a nervous conscience. What a ridiculous idea for a girl to enunciate—a nervous conscience! And actually your aunt only laughed!'

'I laughed at your horrified face, Horace. Of course, Pamela only said it to get a rise out of you. She told me afterwards that there was nothing she loved better. "He looks so splendid when he is angry," she finished.' But this compliment was received by the Vicar with marked disfavour, and Mrs. Glyn, with her usual tact and good-nature, changed the subject.

'I think Gerda is wonderfully improved. She seems to have grown, somehow,' remarked Mr. Glyn, an hour or two later, when their guest had retired.

It was the hour that his wife loved best. The rest of the household were asleep—the long, hard working day was over; but the Vicar still sat by his study fire with his open book before him. Clare always sat opposite to him with her knitting or mending-basket beside her. She knew that in spite of his silence her husband liked to see her there, and at times he would lay down his book or push aside his papers, and tell her the day's troubles or the thoughts that were passing through his mind. And then it would seem to the tired, happy wife as though heaven and earth were very near together, and life a great mystery and sacrament of love. At such times the hesitations and limitations of a difficult, complex nature seemed laid aside like a cloak, and the real Horace Glyn stood revealed to his wife's eyes in his full strength and meaning. 'No one knows him as I do, she would think; and then she would declare to herself, with womanly inconsistency, that he was altogether perfect.

When Mr. Glyn made this remark about Gerda, Clare's eyes glistened with pleasure, and she laid down her work.

'She's a darling!' she returned enthusiastically. 'I always told you she was a fine creature; but oh, Horace! what made you talk so much of Gerard Hamlyn?'

'Is there any reason why I should not talk of him, my dear?' And Mr. Glyn looked at his wife rather keenly.

'She was very much embarrassed when you mentioned his name. I do not know why you should be kept in ignorance, Horace. Honoria wrote to me very fully about him. My father has set his heart on his marrying Gerda, and it appears that Gerard is really in love with her, but Gerda will not have him.'

'Do you mean that she has actually refused him?'

'Yes, indeed. And Honoria tells me that everything is so uncomfortable that the poor child is glad to take refuge with us. I think you ought to know this, Horace, but I have had no opportunity of telling you.'

'Certainly I ought to know it, but, unless Gerda herself speaks to me, you may be sure that I shall not mention the subject. A young girl's confidence is only given to one of her own sex, and unless she has need of priestly counsel she will not speak to me, neither shall I expect her to do so. But, Clare, let her know, if possible, that she has my warmest sympathy. Tell her, if you will, that I honour her for not giving away her heart lightly to this young man, and that she is welcome to stay here as long as she likes.' And Mr. Glyn spoke with decision and energy.

'Thank you, dear; you are very good! I will certainly tell Gerda this when we talk the matter over together; but, Horace, do you know, I feel rather sorry for Gerard. He is such a nice fellow, and Honoria says he is thoroughly in love with her.'

'It will do him no harm,' returned her husband. 'And, after all, the question is for the girl herself to decide. You did not want anyone to help you make up your mind, and you were not older than Gerda when you accepted me.' And a certain softness came over Horace Glyn's features as he remembered how his faithful Clare had given up all for his sake.

'No, Horace, and I have never repented my decision.' And then for a moment a sacred silence fell between the wife and husband.

When the Vicar spoke again it was on a different subject.

'I went to Daintree Road this afternoon, my dear.'

Then Mrs. Glyn roused from her musing fit.

'Did you see Hester?'

'No, she was busy with some music pupils, so I went into the studio. As usual, I found Vincent reading a French novel, with an empty coffee-cup beside him. Upon my word, Clare, I should enjoy horsewhipping the fellow!'

'I quite believe you. Poor Mr. Vincent would have scant mercy at your hands. I suppose Ray was with him?'

'Poor little dear! she was fast asleep on the rug, and he had covered her over with his velvet painting-coat. He apologized for not rising, for fear of waking her, and then he showed me how she had dropped asleep cuddling his boot.'

'I think the best point about him is his love for that child,' observed Clare, secretly touched by this moving picture.

'Do you call it love when he is too lazy to work for her?' returned her husband energetically. 'Of course it was the old excuse—want of light and absence of the model. There were half a dozen pictures, in all stages of progress, and he was sitting by the fire reading Zola.'

'He is very unsatisfactory, certainly. Poor dear Hester! my heart bleeds for her. Did you ask after the boys?'

'There was nothing else to talk about. He says Lyall is paying their school-bills. Harry is really a very clever, intelligent lad, and takes after his mother; but Philip is slower, and does not seem very brilliant.

Would you believe it, Clare, Vincent began inveighing against day-schools for the sons of gentlemen! "They will mix with all the cads of the neighbourhood," he said. "I believe my butcher's son is in the same class with Harry." But I cut him short by asking him who was to send them to a public school; and then he was obliged to confess that he did not see his way to do it. "No one cares about art nowadays," he remarked. I got up and took my leave after that. If I had stayed longer, I should only have quarrelled with him. One must keep the peace, for his wife's sake.'

'Yes, indeed,' agreed his wife, with a sigh; and then she put aside her work-basket, and reminded her husband of the lateness of the hour.

Mrs. Glyn's morning was fully occupied, and Gerda saw little of her until luncheon; so she sat reading in the rocking-chair beside the fire, while Walter prepared his Greek for his tutor, and Bessie wrote out her French translation, or drew in silence. Bessie was completing her education in a somewhat desultory fashion. She explained to Gerda that she and her mother still read history and English literature together, and that she went twice a week to Mrs. Vincent for French and drawing.

'They have a very good French governess, and, of course, Mr. Vincent teaches drawing,' she went on; 'and when father is not too busy, he does a little Euclid and Latin with me.'

'Mouse is a sort of mendicant pupil,' observed Walter, thrusting his fingers through his hair. 'She is thankful for scraps, and gleans stray crumbs of wisdom. Did you ever hear of a girl's education being carried on in such a fashion? She and mother read Macaulay and Green in corners. I am always finding them at it.'

'I am sure I work hard enough,' returned Bessie, much hurt at this flippant speech, 'and mother knows more than most people. I do not know why you always laugh at me, Walter!' and the tears came into Bessie's eyes.

But Walter only laughed again, and shrugged his shoulders.

'Of course a mouse lives on crumbs,' he observed in a teasing voice; but Gerda shook her head at him. She was very fond of Walter, but he must be kept in order. Bessie was a dear good child, and she should not be teased.

'Go on with your Greek, sir,' she said authoritatively, 'and leave poor Bessie alone. What is this that I hear about your going to Oxford? Do you mean that your father can afford to send you there?' and as Gerda spoke, a remembrance of Willie's yellow stockings and thick shoes came to her.

'I never said that he could afford it,' returned Walter rather shortly, and becoming suddenly grave.

'Mother says we shall all be dreadfully stinted,' observed Bessie timidly; but Walter gave her a warning kick.

'You must be very pleased at the prospect,' continued Gerda, in an interested voice, for she and her aunt had often talked for hours about Walter's future career. Clare's son was doubly dear to her since the death of her second boy, and in spite of his reticence the Vicar was very proud of the fine-grown, manly-looking youth who had his mother's eyes.

'I think, if I were a boy, Oxford would be the summit of my ambition,' went on Gerda softly, as she looked out at the chill wintry sunlight. 'I saw it once. It was like a dream of beauty, with its spires and gray old colleges, and its Martyrs' memorial.'

But there was no answering gleam in Walter's eyes.

'I was never there,' he returned shortly. And then he put his elbows on the table, and went back to his Euripides. Gerda felt vaguely that Walter had somehow changed. He was older, and looked more of a man, but he had lost some of his boyish frankness. Perhaps he was busy, and disliked interruption. So she took up her book again.

After luncheon, Mrs. Glyn suggested that they should take their work into the drawing-room. 'It is a raw, chilly afternoon,' she observed; 'and unless you care for a walk, I should gladly be excused.' And as Gerda protested that she was in a lazy mood, and should much enjoy a chat by the fireside, they were soon settled cosily with their work; and long before the twilight had arrived, Mrs. Glyn was in full possession of Gerda's secret.

'I have been so longing to tell you, Aunt

Clare,' she finished. 'I have been so sure of your sympathy all this time. At home they are all for Gerard. No one thinks of me at all in the matter. They think Gerard has only to ask for anything that he wants. Even Doris takes his part.'

'What would you say if I were to take his part too?'

'I should feel as though my last comfort had failed me. Aunt Clare, you are not serious—you do not really think that I ought to marry Gerard?'

'Does it matter so much what I think? Your Uncle Horace is on your side, Gerda. He thinks it very wrong that any such pressure should have been put upon you. As far as that goes, I agree with him. No one has a right to give an opinion in a question of marrying. There are only two people to be considered.'

'Then please do not tell me that you take Gerard's part.'

'No, darling, I will not tell you that—not seriously. But all the same, I am very sorry for Gerard. He is rather a favourite of mine, and I do not like him to be disappointed.'

'Then most certainly you are taking his part.'

'If you tell me that, I will say no more about my sorrow for him. On the contrary, I will put myself in your place, and try and see with your eyes. But you must explain yourself more clearly.'

'Some things are not easy to explain,' returned Gerda sadly. 'They will not resolve themselves into words. Aunt Clare, when you married Uncle Horace, did you feel that, though you loved him, that part of you—your best part—would be starved and left out in the cold?'

'No, child, certainly not. Every thought seemed to belong to him. Do you suppose a divided allegiance would satisfy a man like your uncle?'

'That is for you to say. But, of course, I know all that you gave up for Uncle Horace. If I loved anyone, I would do just the same. I think I would go to the end of the world for such a one. But not with Gerard—no, certainly not with Gerard.'

'Do you mean that you could not trust him?'

'No, Aunt Clare, that is not my meaning. Of course I could trust him wholly. But with all my affection for Gerard, how could I go to the ends of the earth with a man who could not speak my language—who could think none of my thoughts?'

'Ah, I understand you now. There is no part of my mind, as well as my heart, that is not open to my husband. That is a great deal for an old married woman to say.'

'Perhaps so. But, in my opinion, every woman should be able to say the same. People make such terrible mistakes, and they forget that it is for life.'

'You are quite right, dearest. A woman should look up to her husband—not beyond him, or over his head. It is this fatal mistake that has wrecked Hester Vincent's life. She has attained the full stature of her womanhood, and Mr. Vincent is a mere boy still. She has grown and developed since their marriage, but he is just what he always was. They are not on the same plane.'

'Yes, I see. That is very sad. But, Aunt Clare, just let me say one thing before we close the subject. It makes me so happy to know that one person understands me.'

'Then you may be perfectly content.

But, Gerda, surely I know the wearer of that red dress. I am afraid our cosy chat must be brought to an abrupt conclusion. Yes, that is Pamela's knock—she is your first visitor. Just stir the fire into a blaze, that we may be able to see one another's faces.'

CHAPTER XVI.

PAMELA.

'Do not marry a woman whose mouth droops at the corners. Even were the mouth a cherry you would find the fruit bitter.'—CARMEN SYLVA.

'AM I interrupting you, dear people?' exclaimed Pamela, in her usual abrupt fashion, as she advanced into the room. Pamela never came into a room as other people did; she entered with a sudden rush, like a miniature whirlwind. In a moment an energizing influence made itself felt; conversation might be at a low ebb, but in a second it was fanned, reinvigorated, stirred into fresh life and interest. 'You were talking secrets,' she continued, darting an inquisitive glance at Gerda's hot face as she spoke. 'Shall I go away, Mrs. Glyn?—I hate to spoil sport; my good-nature has been my bane all my life—say the word, and I will vanish—dissolve into space!' But Pamela's little feet were planted very firmly on the hearthrug as she spoke.

'Nonsense, Lady-bird! you will just stay where you are,' returned Mrs. Glyn, wheeling up a cosy-looking chair towards the fire. 'I always call her Lady-bird, Gerda, when she wears that red and black dress. So you have come to call on my niece, Pamela? That is very pretty behaviour on your part.'

'It is one of my virtuous days,' returned Pamela placidly. 'I knew when I got out of bed this morning that I should feel good for the remainder of the day: it is rather a nice feeling while it lasts,' she continued meditatively; 'it is a pity that it is so evanescent. So you have come to Cromehurst?' she went on, turning to Gerda. 'I had no idea we should meet so soon;' and her curious, questioning glance made Gerda uncomfortable.

'Yes, it is very soon,' she returned quickly; 'but I had no more idea than you had, Miss Lyall. I always intended to pay Aunt Clare a visit in the summer, but I suddenly saw reason to alter my plans.'

'Indeed!' drawled Pamela. 'Well, never mind the reasons, they are no business of mine—everyone has a right to his or her own mysteries. I am very glad to see you, Miss Meredith; we got on very well together at Chesterton, and I know we shall soon be fast friends. You are looking paler and thinner; I suppose that has something to do with the mysteries, too.'

'Pamela,' observed Mrs. Glyn significantly, 'if you are going to make invidious remarks, I shall not ask you to take off your hat and jacket and spend the evening with us.'

'I could not do it under any circumstances, madam. I always call Mrs. Glyn "madam" when she presumes to lecture your humble servant. I have a particular engagement this evening.'

'I suppose Mr. Vincent is coming?'

'I see no reason to deny the fact. Yes, Derrick is coming to dinner; but as it is by his own invitation, not mine, I will throw him over if you like.'

'You will do nothing of the kind, Ladybird!'

And then Pamela laughed mischievously.

'I have half a mind to do it—only it would be punishing myself as well as Derrick; and as I have not seen him for five weeks, I have so much to say to him. I don't believe we shall have a pleasant evening, as Alick is in a bad temper. We quarrelled at breakfast-time this morning.'

'Oh, indeed! I understood this was one of your virtuous days, Pamela?'

But Pamela took this little rebuff quite sweetly.

'Exactly so; and that proves how wrong and unreasonable Alick must be. Would you believe it, Mrs. Glyn: he scolded me dreadfully just because I had given our cook warning!'

'You have given Rebecca warning?'

'Certainly I have!' in a tone of indignant innocence. 'Alick has been complaining lately that the joints are overdone. He has spoken several times about it; and I talked very seriously to Rebecca. With all her good points, Rebecca is a little short in her temper; and, I am sorry to say, she answered me very rudely, and then I told her that she must go. And now Jane has given warning, too. That is the worst of having sisters: I always told Alick it would not answer.'

Mrs. Glyn threw a comical glance of dismay across at her niece.

'They were two of the nicest girls in Cromehurst. I have known them for years,' she observed pathetically.

'That is just what Alick said this morning. He was as angry with me as possible. He said I had no right to take such a step without consulting him; that he was the master of the house, and so on. And then he declared that he should ask Rebecca to stay.'

'I hope he will; but all the same, it will be very unpleasant for you, Pamela.'

'Do you think I do not know that?' and Pamela's eyes had a naughty flash in them. 'Rebecca will stay just to spite me, and she and Jane will be quietly insolent every day of their lives. I told Alick that if he carried out his threat I should wash my hands of the whole business, and that he could manage the house himself. And what do you think he was rude enough to say? That the house would be better managed, and that, on the whole, he thought me the worst housekeeper that a man could have.'

'Oh, come! that is rather too severe on you, Pamela;' and Mrs. Glyn looked kindly at her favourite, and Gerda observed in a low voice that she was quite sure Dr. Lyall did not mean it.

'You are wrong, Miss Meredith; Alick meant every word he said. He has gone off to Hester now, to talk over his troubles. This is what always happens. Hester will listen to him, and then she will give him advice and comfort him. She will tell him to speak to Rebecca, and give all the orders himself. When I go home, Jane will open the door to me, and there will be a gleam of malicious triumph in her eyes; and then Alick will send for me into the study, and tell me, in a cold, sarcastic voice, that he intends that both the servants shall stay, and that for the future he hopes I shall do nothing without consulting him. Oh, we have had these little scenes a score of times before — have we not, Mrs. Glyn? — and Hester is always the peacemaker.'

'I wish you were more like her, Pamela;' and Mrs. Glyn shook her head indulgently. 'I am really very sorry for Dr. Lyall—he does so like a quiet life, and to have things comfortable and orderly about him. If it were not for Hester, I hardly know what he would do.'

Pamela heaved a deep sigh.

'" Et tu, Brute!" ' she exclaimed reproachfully. 'No one has a good word for me. When I confide in Derrick this evening, he will tell me to my face that it is all my fault. No one understands me, Miss Meredith. Alick treats me as though I were a naughty child, and my *fiancé* laughs at me, and refuses to take my part; and even Mrs. Glyn has not a kind word for me.' But though Pamela spoke quite seriously, and there was a suspicious moisture in her bright eyes, Mrs. Glyn only seemed amused.

'I begin to think you are incorrigible,' she returned; 'and if Gerda were not sitting opposite to us, I should treat you to a lecture myself. I am very fond of you, Pamela, but, all the same, you are a very faulty little person.'

Pamela made a face at her, and such a droll, whimsical expression crossed her features, that Gerda could not help laughing, and in an instant Pamela recovered her good temper.

'That is right, Miss Meredith, you are just like me—you see the humorous side of everything. In spite of my vexation, I nearly burst out laughing in Alick's face this morning, he did look so ridiculously solemn. After all, life is too short for these misunderstandings. It is not in my nature to bear malice. Before many hours are over, I shall have forgiven Alick, and we shall be the best of friends. Now let us talk of something else. How long are you going to stay at Cromehurst?'

'I shall keep her just as long as I can,' returned Mrs. Glyn, glancing at the clock. 'Now I must leave you for half an hour, while I write a letter for my husband, and then we shall have some tea. You are in no hurry, Pamela?'

'Not in the least. I suppose Alick has ordered the dinner, or Derrick will fare badly. Not that I mean to trouble my head about it. I shall fortify myself with tea and cake, and then I shall be prepared for any emergency. You look shocked, Miss Meredith—must I go on calling you Miss Meredith? But everything is fair in love and war, and just now I am waging war with my dearly beloved brother.'

'Yes; but your warfare does not extend to Mr. Vincent?'

'Humph! I am not so sure of that. I will tell you a secret, Miss Meredith. Derrick and I are not an orthodox couple—we are getting over all our quarrels before the happy day arrives—if it ever does arrive;' and here a cloudy look came over Pamela's face.

'I think a long engagement must be rather nice,' observed Gerda. 'One would get to know a person so thoroughly.'

'Oh, that is all very well in theory,' returned Pamela impatiently; 'but I do not agree with you in the least. To a person of my excitable temperament, a long engagement is the most exasperating thing in the world.'

'If this be really your opinion, I wonder you were ever engaged.'

'Well, I would not have been if Derrick had not asked me.' And Pamela blushed very prettily. 'I suppose we poor girls must just submit to our destiny. I tell Derrick he must have bewitched me. Take warning by me, Miss Meredith, and avoid that treacherous pitfall that Man—spelt with a big capital—spreads for the unwary and innocent victim—Man the deceiver, the ruthless destroyer of feminine peace and freedom.'

'Please don't be so tragical,' returned Gerda, laughing. And then, as the subject was a delicate one, and there was a touch of concealed bitterness in Pamela's mocking tones, she skilfully changed the topic to one of more general interest, which lasted until Mrs. Glyn returned, followed by her husband.

Mr. Glyn looked rather stiff and dignified as he took up his favourite position on the rug, but Pamela nodded to him with great friendliness.

'I have turned up again, like a bad penny,' she remarked pleasantly. 'That is the best of a Vicarage—it is neutral ground—and one's Vicar is bound to be civil to his parishioners, however much he dislikes them. I am one of the lambs of your flock, Mr. Glyn, and if my fleece is not as white as it should be, it is your duty to watch over me.' But Mr. Glyn only frowned over this playful speech, and tried to snub his irrepressible guest by asking Gerda how she had spent the afternoon.

But it was not easy to snub Pamela.

'Do you know, Mr. Glyn,' she observed presently, when he handed her some cake,

'I have had scruples of conscience about idleness lately. I belong to the unemployed—to the drones of life—and it is quite time for me to be a busy, busy bee. I want you to allot me a district.'

'Now, Pamela,' remonstrated Mrs. Glyn, from the tea-table, 'be a good lassie for once.' But Pamela refused to take this gentle hint.

'Of course, you do not believe I am serious,' wrinkling her brows at the Vicar as she spoke; 'but I assure you I am quite in earnest. I have got tired of improving my mind, and I think it is high time to turn my talents to account. Now, a district will just give me the employment I want. I am fond of talking, and I like to mix with my fellow-creatures. And I get on very well with old men, and old women too'—evidently an after-thought. 'Of course, if they were ill, you would not expect me to visit them.'

'Oh, I see,' remarked Mr. Glyn dryly. 'I am sorry to tell you, Miss Lyall, that I have no vacant district to allot to you. If you want employment, you might take a class in our schools, and help Miss Lingard.' But Pamela shook her head with an air of disgust.

'Miss Lingard, the infant-school mistress! No, thank you, Mr. Glyn; that is not at all the work I should choose. I was never very partial to children, even when they were tolerably clean and well-behaved. But infants from Elm-tree Road and Hazelbeech Gardens are odious.'

'Uncle Horace,' interposed Gerda hurriedly, as she saw a gathering blackness on Mr. Glyn's brow, 'I shall be very pleased to help Miss Lingard. I have often taken a class in the schools, and I think the work will just suit me.'

'Thank you, my dear. I shall gladly avail myself of your offer. Miss Lingard's mother is dying, and I am anxious to spare her as much as possible. Perhaps, if you and Bessie were to offer your services to-morrow——'

'It must be in the morning, then,' observed Mrs. Glyn, 'for Hester has asked me to bring Gerda to see her. It is a half-holiday, and she will be at leisure. Shall we see you there, Pamela?'

'I think not,' returned Pamela, buttoning her gloves with some dignity. 'I shall give Daintree Road a wide berth for the present.

Good-bye, Miss Meredith! I shall expect you to return this visit very soon. Mrs. Glyn will show you the way to Roadside—Bessie, you may come too, if you like. Good-evening, Mr. Glyn! I am sorry that you will not have me for one of your workers. I shall have to offer my valuable services to Mr. Higginbotham instead.'

Now, the Rev. Joseph Higginbotham was the incumbent of an iron church that had recently been erected. He belonged to the Evangelical school, and of late there had been some passages of arms between him and the Vicar of St. Jude's.

'Perhaps there may be refuge for the stray lamb at St. Barnabas's,' she continued, smiling sweetly at the Vicar as she spoke. 'Do you know, Alick attends Mrs. Higginbotham and all the little Higginbothams, so they have a sort of claim on us;' and then Pamela smiled again, and whisked out of the room, to be followed and scolded by Mrs. Glyn.

'You are a naughty child, Pamela!' she said in a vexed voice. 'Whatever made you drag in Mr. Higginbotham's name? He and Horace are at daggers drawn. Mr.

Higginbotham was most insulting at the vestry meeting.'

'He is a good little man, and preaches sound doctrine,' returned Pamela obstinately, 'and if Mr. Glyn refuse my services——'

'But, Pamela, it is such nonsense; you are not in the least fitted for district work; you have no idea how strict Horace is with his workers, and yet they are all so devoted to him. You do not mean to say you were really serious?' as she caught sight of Pamela's face.

'Yes, I was,' with a little catch in her voice, that sounded like a sob; 'but no one believes in me. Alick is always telling me that I do nothing for my fellow-creatures, and life is so dull and stupid. And then there is Derrick always on one's mind.'

'Oh, I see,' returned Mrs. Glyn in a soothing tone, as though she were talking to an infant; 'but Mr. Vincent will soon put it all straight. Things have gone wrong to-day, and you are a little down-hearted; but Mr. Higginbotham and St. Barnabas will not mend matters. If you like, you shall help me in my district; there is such a dear old man—an ex-policeman—who is crippled with rheumatism, and wants someone to read the paper to him;' and then Pamela brightened up and went off quite comforted.

'Pamela was really in earnest, Horace,' observed Mrs. Glyn, when she went back to the drawing-room; 'she is a little bit low in her mind, and wants occupation. I have promised to find her something to do in Acacia Road.'

Mr. Glyn shrugged his shoulders. 'Very well, my dear, you can do as you like. If you choose to introduce quicksilver into your district, you must take the consequences; but I shall not envy you your experience;' and then he went off to his study.

'It is such a pity Miss Lyall and Uncle Horace get on so badly together,' began Gerda, as the door closed after him. 'I am afraid he rather dislikes her than otherwise. What sort of a man is Mr. Vincent? I asked Uncle Horace just now, and he said he was far too good for her.'

'He is certainly very nice, though he is not at all handsome. He is a very big man, and Pamela looks such a tiny creature beside him. He is just her opposite, Gerda: he is placid and even-tempered, and talks very well.'

'Aunt Clare, I do not think Miss Lyall is quite happy in her engagement.'

'Why do you not call her Pamela?—most people do. I think you are mistaken; she is very fond of Derrick Vincent, and I am quite sure nothing would induce her to give him up. He is perfectly devoted to her. You have seen Pamela in an unfortunate mood to-day: everything has gone wrong, and she and her brother have had a serious quarrel; but even in her naughty tempers Pamela is interesting.'

'All the same, I am inclined to pity Mr. Vincent;' and then Gerda put away her work and went to her room.

CHAPTER XVII.

'WITH DR. AND MISS LYALL'S COMPLIMENTS.'

'Neither in writing nor in reading wilt thou be able to lay down rules for others before thou shalt have first learned to obey rules thyself. Much more is this in life.'—M. AURELIUS ANTONINUS.

GERDA kept her promise, and directly after breakfast the next morning she and Bessie went to the infant school. On their way home she had promised to do some shopping for Mrs. Glyn, and Bessie had willingly accompanied her. It was always a pleasure to Gerda to walk through the town; there was something quaint and picturesque in the gray old houses interspersed between the shops; and she liked to stand on Crown Hill and look down Conduit Street at the old tower of the parish church, flanked by its guardian poplars. The old adage, that distance lends enchantment to the view, was certainly true in this case. A nearer inspection of Conduit Street, with its mean, unsavoury shops, its shabby furniture-dealers and purveyors of old clothes, would have failed to excite even a passing interest; but from Crown Hill the steep, narrow street wore a different aspect. There was a sense of breezy distance—a breadth of sky-line, with soft cloudy effects, the rooks circling round the poplars; and the church-tower seemed to invest the scene with interest: one forgot the shabby wares on either side of the street, to think rather pitifully of the aged lives that wore so peacefully to their close in the modest almshouses below.

'If I were rich, I would rather build almshouses than churches,' observed Gerda, as they lingered to look at an old bookstall. 'Don't look so shocked, Bessie; you remind me of Doris when you open your eyes like that. I love churches quite as much as you do, but we are not all called upon to do such great work, and I have always been so fond of old people. It breaks my heart to see the poor old creatures in workhouses, without their little comforts and their warm corners.

They have worked so hard all their lives, and it is no fault of theirs if their poor old limbs lose power, or get crippled with rheumatism.'

'I have heard mother talk in much the same way,' returned Bessie quietly. She was not sufficiently at her ease with her clever cousin to venture to air her own opinions, and few people guessed at the strength and decision of character which lay under the timid, shrinking manner.

'Aunt Clare and I think alike on most points,' returned Gerda quickly. 'Don't you see, Bessie, hardship does not seem to matter when one is young and strong—the back is fitted for the burden; but the old are so weak, they are like little children in their helplessness: they want sunshine, kindness, a corner by their own fireside, a hand held out to them now and then. That is why I should like to build almshouses, to keep them safe and warm until they are called home.'

'Oh yes, I see what you mean,' returned Bessie; and then she added, with a sort of effort, 'It is a pity that old Mrs. Chalmers and Mrs. Horsfall bicker so dreadfully. Father had to interfere once. Mrs. Chalmers was so spiteful. She slopped all over poor Mrs. Horsfall's floor one day, just as she had cleaned it. Mrs. Chalmers said her foot slipped, and her pail tipped over, but no one believes it; it was just spitefulness on account of the grocery tickets.'

'My dear child, human nature is imperfect, even in almshouses; but I hope Mrs. Chalmers is an exception. Why, who is that gentleman?'—as Bessie coloured and bowed to a good-looking young man who was wheeling a child's perambulator on the other side of the street. Gerda had noticed him before Bessie had given that sign of recognition. She had wondered who that striking-looking man could be. There was something out of the common and picturesque about him; he looked rather like a foreigner, with his olive complexion and fur-lined coat, and there was something incongruous in his homely employment: one might as well have expected to see a Bond Street lounger wheeling home a truck of clean clothes.

'That is Mr. Vincent,' returned Bessie in a low voice. 'He is crossing the road. I think he wants to speak to us. Do you mind waiting a moment, Gerda?'

'Do you mean Mr. Julius Vincent? Of course I do not mind;' and then both girls watched the skilful propelling of the perambulator between a coal-cart and a waggon. Most people would have hesitated to cross Crown Hill at that moment, but Mr. Vincent seemed to have no scruple. He held up his hand as a caution to an omnibus-driver, and shook his head reproachfully at a cabman, before he and his charge were landed safely on the pavement.

'A thousand apologies for keeping you two ladies waiting,' observed Mr. Vincent, raising his hat; 'but I was on my way to St. Jude's Vicarage with a note from my wife; and then Ray suddenly discovered she was cold and hungry, and that we must go home at once. Between my two liege ladies, I was in sorry plight, until I caught sight of you, Miss Bessie, and then I resolved to throw myself on your goodness.'

'I will certainly take your note, Mr. Vincent. Poor little Ray! She looks quite blue with cold.'

'She does indeed,' murmured Gerda, with a pitying look at the child's pale face. There was something painfully pathetic in the melancholy dark eyes and thin, drawn features under the big hood, which told their own sad tale of suffering. There is always something unnatural in the idea of a mere infant struggling with some cruel chronic disease. It would have been a beautiful little face, Gerda thought, but for the sharp lines and grave, unsmiling eyes.

'Ray wants to go home, dada,' observed the child fretfully.

'And you shall go home, my darling,' returned Mr. Vincent tenderly. 'Dada is a naughty, naughty man to take Ray out in the cold. Ray must whip him with her new little whip when she gets home, until he cries out.—Miss Bessie, I am your debtor from this day. Good-morning, ladies. There has been no introduction, but I presume this is your cousin, Miss Meredith?—Now then, Beauty bright, for the whip!' and the next moment he was propelling the perambulator across Crown Hill.

'What a strange man!' observed Gerda; 'but he is really very handsome—and how young he looks! there is something almost boyish in his manner. It seems such a droll idea, wheeling that perambulator.'

'Oh, he always does it,' returned Bessie; 'and no one thinks anything of it at Cromehurst. It is just Mr. Vincent's way to do odd things. I believe Ray refuses to go out with anyone else. He has spoilt her dreadfully, and now he's a perfect slave to her whims. Ray is much fonder of him than she is of her mother; but, then, poor Mrs. Vincent is too busy to attend to her.'

'It seems rather a strange household,' returned her cousin. 'From all accounts, Mrs. Vincent and her husband have reversed the usual order of things: she is the breadwinner, and he takes the part of nurse. One can hardly understand the position.'

'You will understand it when you go there,' replied Bessie rather sadly. 'Mr. Vincent is very good-natured, but he fritters away his time dreadfully; and there is so little real work done, that poor Mrs. Vincent is obliged to put her shoulder to the wheel. Someone must work, you know. He gives drawing-lessons, but people are afraid to have him: they say he is too handsome and flighty in manner to be safe with girls; but mother says that is nonsense, and that there is no harm in him.'

This was a long speech for Bessie, but she evidently shared her father's opinion of Mr. Vincent, and had scant patience with the fascinating Julius. Gerda felt both curious and interested. She longed to see this wonderful Mrs. Vincent—the Hester who was her uncle Horace's ideal, and for whom Aunt Clare felt such warm affection. And then, by some subtle connection of ideas, she wondered if any of Dr. Lyall's patients lived in the town. It was strange to think that any moment they might meet him. She longed to ask Bessie if he walked or drove; they were passing Dr. Brown's house at that moment, and a doctor's brougham with a bay mare was standing at the door.

'I thought Dr. Brown drove a pair of gray horses?' she observed carelessly—and the bait took.

'So he does,' returned Bessie innocently; 'that is Dr. Lyall's brougham. He told mother the other day that he could not well afford a carriage until his practice increased, but the long distances obliged him to keep one. It is rather a shabby brougham, but, then, Dr. Lyall does not care about appearances.

'I dare say not,' was the brief answer, and then Gerda grew a little absent.

Her colour rose slightly when, by-and-by, she heard wheels behind them. She hardly ventured to look round as the brougham passed them. She slackened her pace involuntarily as it stopped again before a house, and Dr. Lyall descended. Evidently he had not seen them: he went up the steps quickly and let himself in; it must be his own house, but Gerda never glanced at it as she went by. She felt a little chilled—disappointed. Could it be possible that, after all, he had seen them and avoided recognition? He knew of her arrival—she had been two whole days in the place; and of course Pamela had called on her. After all, why should she torment herself in this way? He was reading his paper—doctors always read their paper—why need he stare at every passer-by? He might be absorbed in thought of some critical operation, or perhaps one of his patients was worse—dying. Doctors must be different from other men; they went from one sick-bed to another; their life was so crowded with interest, such awful interest, it was no wonder they could pass their friends without seeing them.

Gerda felt a little comforted when she arrived at this point, but she was a trifle restless, and her uncle's discourse at luncheon fell on deaf ears; she only roused into animation when Mrs. Glyn spoke of their afternoon visit.

'Should you mind going very early?' she asked. 'If we are fashionable, and arrive about tea-time, we shall have to put up with Mr. Vincent's society, and I think we women would like a little chat by ourselves first.'

'No one would doubt that for a moment, my dear,' replied Mr. Glyn dryly, as he rose from the table—which was rather unhandsome on the Vicar's part, as he had kept the conversation in his own hands for the last half-hour; 'I think a woman would rather go without her food than without talking.'

But Mrs. Glyn was not to be damped by her husband's sarcasm.

'When Hester and I get together, we have a real interesting talk,' she returned brightly. 'You need not shake your head, Horace; men like gossip just as well as we do; and I expect there is plenty of small-talk at the clubs.'

'Aunt Clare,' interrupted Gerda mischievously, 'do you remember Lord Houghton's famous speech? "There is nothing so wearying as continually playing at superiority." There is a great deal of preaching at us poor women folk; but I expect the men talk scandal too.'

'Pax, pax!' returned Mr. Glyn, with a gesture as though he were brushing off some noxious insect; 'one woman is enough for me to manage. Have your own way, my dear, as long as I am not obliged to hear your conversation. I will put no veto upon it; Eve's daughters have all a strong family likeness,' and with this scathing remark the Vicar retired to his study to prepare himself for his afternoon's labours.

'I think I shall get to like Uncle Horace in time,' thought Gerda, as she went up to her room; 'he is dictatorial, but he is not nearly so severe as he used to be: he is more careful of other people's feelings.'

Gerda was surprised to find that they would have to pass Roadside again on their way to Daintree Road; but this time she ventured on a glance. It was rather a high, narrow house, and only an area railing separated it from the pavement. A flight of steps led to the door, and the windows had wire blinds to ensure privacy.

'You must not judge from the outside,' observed Mrs. Glyn, as though she feared some deprecating remark. 'Roadside is not a modern house, but it is really very comfortable, and its low rent induced Dr. Lyall to take it. The two windows on the left belong to the dining-room, and the study is on the other side ; Pamela's drawing-room is upstairs. Ah, here comes the little lady ! I believe she was on the watch for us.'

Pamela came down the steps with great dignity. She had two little notes in her hand, which she delivered with great solemnity. 'For Mrs. Glyn and Miss Meredith, with Dr. and Miss Lyall's compliments,' she lisped—Pamela had an engaging little lisp when she chose. And then she turned, as though to go up the steps again ; but Mrs. Glyn detained her.

'What does this mean, Pamela ?—not an invitation to dinner, I hope.'

'You must not be too sanguine, Mrs. Glyn ; you will find it all correct. "Dr. and Miss Lyall request the pleasure, etc.—R.S.V.P." I got printed cards on purpose. Shall I walk with you to the corner of Daintree Road?' she continued: 'cart-ropes would not drag me farther. I do love a nice biting east wind; it seems to put life into one. I shall go for a five-mile walk, and think of my sins. I am half inclined to fetch Jessie Brown, just by way of penance, only I dare not trust my temper.'

'Pamela,' interrupted Mrs. Glyn reprovingly, as she read the note, 'there was no need for all this ceremony. I meant to ask you and your brother to come in one evening; but why should you put yourselves to such trouble? My husband has not a single evening free for the next week, and I hardly like to leave him.'

'You and Alick must settle that between you,' returned Pamela indifferently. 'I have had my orders, and I am carrying them out. There has been a grand scene of reconciliation, and I am on my best behaviour. I think the meagre diet yesterday had a salutary effect on my high and mighty brother, for he condescended to ask me to show him the intended bill of fare. But it was still simmering in my brain. "If you are a good girl, Pam, and give us a decent dinner, you may have Derrick down." Was not that a bribe ?'

'Did they fare so very badly yesterday ?' asked Mrs. Glyn anxiously; and Pamela's eyes sparkled with naughty fun.

'Well, it was a cold night, you see, and a leg of mutton on the third day is never very inviting; but there were pickles—plenty of pickles—and with bread and cheese——'

'Pamela, how could you be so unfeeling! It was really barbarous treatment to those poor tired men,' really waxing a little warm in her sympathy. 'It was carrying a joke too far — it was almost ill-natured.' But Pamela took this outburst with surprising meekness.

'I think I must call for Jessie Brown,' she observed with a deep sigh, 'or the fruits of repentance will be wanting. What a pity both Mr. Glyn and Mr. Higginbotham disapprove of auricular confession—it would be such a comfortable ordinance to a sinner like myself.'

'Pamela, do not be irreverent!' And then, after a moment's reflection, 'I rather wonder at Dr. Lyall. I should have thought last night's experience would have prevented his inviting anyone to dinner for a long time.'

'Oh dear no! Besides, I promised faithfully that such a thing should never happen again. Well, here we are at Daintree Road. Give my love to Hester;' and Pamela nodded to them both, and whisked round the corner.

'Aunt Clare,' asked Gerda in a dubious tone, 'do you not think that Pamela treats her brother very badly?'

'I think I shall decline to answer that question. I am afraid they are rather an ill-assorted couple to live together. Pamela ought to have married, and Hester should have kept her brother's house. Things always went smoothly in the old times—he has told me so over and over again. "When Hester married, I had no more home comfort," he said once. It is my belief that Pamela is really devoted to her brother, and that in some way he repels and disappoints her. She is a most exacting little person, and all this flightiness and nonsense is her mode of taking revenge. If only Dr. Lyall could afford a wife! but Hester's unlucky marriage has only added to his responsibilities. He is one of the best brothers—indeed, one of the best men I know.' And with this splendid eulogium on Dr. Lyall, Mrs. Glyn paused at the gate of a large old-fashioned house, standing rather far back from the road, with 'Establishment for Young Ladies' on a glittering brass plate.

END OF VOL. I.

BILLING AND SONS, PRINTERS, GUILDFORD.
G., C. & Co.

www.ingramcontent.com/pod-product-compliance
Lightning Source LLC
Chambersburg PA
CBHW021202230426
43667CB00006B/523